Preparing Educators to Communicate and Connect with Families and Communities

A volume in
Literacy, Language, and Learning
Series Editor: Patricia Ruggiano Schmidt

Preparing Educators to Communicate and Connect with Families and Communities

Edited by

Patricia Ruggiano Schmidt
Le Moyne College

INFORMATION AGE
PUBLISHING

80 Mason Street • Greenwich, Connecticut 06830 • www.infoagepub.com

Library of Congress Cataloging-in-Publication Data

Preparing educators to communicate and connect with families and
communities / edited by Patricia Ruggiano Schmidt.
  p. cm. – (Language, literacy, and learning)
  Includes bibliographical references.
  ISBN 1-59311-324-2 (pbk.) – ISBN 1-59311-325-0 (hardcover)
  1. Parent-teacher relationships–New York (State)–Case studies. 2.
Home and school–New York (State)–Case studies. 3. Community and
school–New York (State)–Case studies. 4. Communication in
education–New York (State)–Case studies. I. Schmidt, Patricia
Ruggiano, 1944- II. Series.
  LC225.32.N7P74 2005
  371.102'2–dc22

                                                                    2005001682

These materials were created by members of the Initiative 12 Study Group, Preparing
Teachers to Engage with Families, with funding from the U.S. Department of Education
awarded to Syracuse University's New York Higher Education Support Center for System-
sChange under Grant #H027A020104, CFDA #84.027 to the New York State Education
Department, Office of Vocational and Educational Services to Individuals with Disabilities. The opinions expressed herein are those of the authors and no endorsement by the
New York State Education Department or Syracuse University should be inferred.

Printed in the United States of America

ACKNOWLEDGMENTS

This product was created through the collaborative efforts of the Initiative 12 Study Group, Preparing Teachers to Engage with Families. We would like to thank the members of this study group for their insight, contributions, authorship, and peer review of this guide, and for their dedication to excellence. The members include:

Ellen Chernoff—*Teacher In-service Staff Development*—*Capital Region BOCES*
Amanda Fenlon—*Assistant Professor*—*SUNY Oswego*
Grace Ibanez Friedman—*Assistant Professor*—*St. John's University*
Diane Heller—*Parent*—*Syracuse City School District*
Peter Kozik—*School Administrator and Doctoral Student*—*Syracuse University*
Tracy Knight Lackey—*Assistant Professor*—*Syracuse University*
Marybeth A. Schillace—*Parent advocate and teacher*
Patricia Ruggiano Schmidt—*Literacy Professor*—*Le Moyne College*

We thank Melissa Price, Project Coordinator for New York Higher Education Support Center for Systems Change at Syracuse University, for her constant support and encouragement throughout the process of creating this document. She attended meetings and demonstrated great interest in our work...every step of the way.

We thank Steven Kulick, Le Moyne College Director of Corporate and Foundation Relations, for his profound interest in every aspect of the project. His timely reports and ability to help us at a moment's notice helped us stay positive.

We are grateful to our editors, Jim and Connie Sullivan, Sullivan Educational Associates, for their thoughtful, thorough, and knowledgeable work on this project. Due to their positive analysis, the readability and organization of the text have been enhanced.

CONTENTS

APPENDICES

FOREWORD

Preparing Educators to Communicate and Connect with Families and Communities

Patricia A. Edwards
Professor of Language & Literacy
Michigan State University

It is no secret to Patricia Ruggiano Schmidt that "common sense ideas, legislation and educational research" reveals that family involvement is critical to the academic achievement of children. Similarly, it is no secret to her that the responsibility for preparing teachers to work with families falls squarely on the shoulders of teacher educators (Williams, 1992, Edwards, 2004). What is baffling to her is "why isn't this collaboration happening in all schools? What are the major stumbling blocks for achieving this necessary collaboration? How do we develop collaboration among families, community members, and school staff?" Schmidt is one of those innovative teacher educators who decided not to wait for somebody else to answer this series of questions that she cares so deeply about. Instead she applied and received a grant to seek answers to these important questions.

This unique and visionary text is a compilation of fascinating case studies by New York State teachers, parents and professors. These down-to-

Preparing Educators to Communicate and Connect with Families and Communities, pages ix–x
Copyright © 2005 by Information Age Publishing
All rights of reproduction in any form reserved.

earth case studies highlight effective specific approaches to provide bridges between home and school and a look to the future for preparing teachers to communicate and connect with families and communities.

This book promises to make a significant contribution to preparing teachers to engage all families and communities in the education of our children. It is filled with thoughtful activities coming out of an incredible body of educational research done by the contributors. This book has given us the answers to the questions that Schmidt raised and it will move family involvement from high rhetoric to high practice. This book will change the way we prepare teachers and it is a must read for those in teacher education programs. As teachers, parents, and teacher educators, we are in Schmidt's debt.

REFERENCE

Edwards, P. A. (2004). *Children's literacy development: Making it happen through school, family, and community involvement.* Boston, MA: Allyn and Bacon.

Williams, Jr., D. L. (1992). Parental involvement in teacher preparation: Challenges to teacher education. In L. Kaplan (Ed.), *Education and the family* (pp. 243–254). Boston, MA: Allyn and Bacon.

PREFACE

The Problem and Process

Patricia Ruggiano Schmidt
Literacy Professor—Le Moyne College

In this media-driven, fast-paced society, much sage advice from the past seems forgotten:

> "We are all connected."
> "It takes a village to educate a child."
> "Our children are the nation's most important natural resource.
> We must all invest in their future."

These are just a few common sense statements proclaiming the necessity for collaboration in the education of our children. Unfortunately, though, it is recognized that there are serious discrepancies between educators' preparation for family-community involvement and expectations for their home-school-community connections (Shartrand, Weiss, & Lopez, 1997). Under the Federal *No Child Left Behind* law, parental involvement and participation for the social, emotional, and academic growth of children is strongly supported. Additionally, research strongly suggests that schools and classrooms that reach out to collaborate with families and communities have children who learn and thrive (Heath, 1983; Trueba, Jacobs, & Kirton, 1990; Ladson-Billings, 1994, 1995; Edwards, 2004). Simi-

Preparing Educators to Communicate and Connect with Families and Communities, pages xi–xvi
Copyright © 2005 by Information Age Publishing
All rights of reproduction in any form reserved.

larly, family members who are comfortable in the schools and are partners with decision making bodies in the schools have children who know success in the schools (Boykin, 1984; Goldenberg, 1987; Moll, 1992; Nieto, 1996; Walker-Dalhouse & Dalhouse, 2001; Edwards, 2004). So, if we recognize the significance of these common sense ideas, legislation, and educational research, why isn't this collaboration happening in all schools? What are the major stumbling blocks for achieving this necessary collaboration? How do we develop collaboration among families, community members, and school staff?

We, the teachers, parents, and professors who shared all aspects of creating this document, believe collaboration for our children's education is a priority. We believe that educators who learn to reach out and communicate with families and communities will most certainly become agents of change in their schools. As we collaborated, we became passionate about our work for children. Therefore, we decided to state our message clearly, at the very beginning of this document.

- We believe that teacher preparation programs and in-service programs should be devoted to the idea that educators are crucial elements in the development of effective communication between home and school, and community and school.
- We believe that teachers must be prepared for multiple communication strategies. They must be willing to reach out to diverse populations with attitudes that respect and appreciate differences regarding physical, cognitive, emotional, linguistic, cultural, ethnic, and economic factors of their students, families and communities.
- We believe that teachers and administrators should be supported and mentored as they are prepared to engage family and community members. Opportunities for modeling and observing need to be available for successful implementation of the ideas related to reaching out and connecting with families and communities.
- We believe that successful schools have blurred the boundaries between home and school and have dissolved the power issues that prevent collaboration for children's education.

Considering the tenets related to common sense, legislation, and research, the purpose of this document is to help present and future teachers think about and implement successful ideas of the past and present to better educate our children. We believe we have a framework in this document for engaging families in a partnership for the education of their children. We hope that teacher and administrator certification programs and in-service school district programs will find our work important and helpful, since we actually experienced the satisfactions associated with educational collaborative efforts. We are pleased with this text and believe the process we experienced should be briefly explained.

OUR PROCESS

We were a group of eight that consisted of self-selected New York State teachers, parents, and professors who applied and received a grant. Initially, most of us did not know each other personally or professionally. One of us who applied was named facilitator by the reviewers of the grant. Our first meeting was a daylong session where we began talking face-to-face about the research on home, school, and community collaboration. We also shared personal experiences related to family engagement and the educational process and prepared a timeline for the year. The grant required that we study the following first four subtopics; we added the fifth.

1. Ways in which teachers may incorporate the cultural and social contributions of a family into schools.
2. Ways in which teachers may learn to communicate and respond to families.
3. Ways to ascertain and influence teacher disposition to family engagement.
4. Ways in which teachers empower families to interact with the school as collaborators in the educational process.
5. Ways in which educational leadership can initiate and encourage collaboration among all partners in the process of educating our children.

Initially, we decided to systematically collect, share, read, and analyze articles related to research and practice. We used e-mail and telephone for the exchange of ideas, questions, and comments and had a total of six daylong meetings throughout the year. Writing began at the third meeting and was divided among the group members' individual interests. As we wrote, revised, and edited, we posted our work on an Internet blackboard. Discussion of published research, unpublished case studies, as well as personal stories were part of all meetings. We all contributed to the creation of the final document and came to know and respect each other's diverse perspectives. However, we soon realized we had one major unifying theme that served as a foundation for all of our beliefs about family engagement:

Teachers who are prepared to reach out and engage families and community members for the education of their children will certainly make a difference.

As a result, these teachers will see the family and community contributions that can be integrated into the curriculum and bring relevancy to learning.

We wanted to assist present and future teachers as they learned to do just that.

ORGANIZATION OF THE TEXT

This document is organized according to the above-mentioned five topics. Each topic will begin with a case study and follow with a brief summary of related research. Then successful strategies will be outlined for present and future educators to adapt and implement. This document will validate many of the ideas teacher educators, teachers, administrators, and parents believe are important and add many new ideas to the preparation of present and future educators to work with families and community.

Section One, *Home-to-School Communication,* involves a case study of communication gone awry. Grace Ibanez Friedman, Assistant Professor in the Education Department at St. John's University, learns about teacher/parent communication with multiple interpretations of data that demonstrate the complexities of making successful connections for home-school-community collaboration. Dr. Friedman sets the tone for this document, explaining that communication is challenging but critical to the successful education of our children. She leaves the reader with many considerations and many helpful ideas for developing communication.

Section Two, *Ascertaining and Influencing Pre-service Teacher Disposition(s) to Family Engagement,* by Tracy Knight Lackey, Assistant Professor of Education at Syracuse University, describes the many ways we can determine the disposition of educators for communicating with our diverse student populations. This is important for teacher educators to understand as they attempt to develop programs to change and reinforce attitudes, which will help present and future teachers reach out to families and communities for children's academic achievement. She gives us several specific ways to determine dispositions and ways to actually change negative attitudes.

Section Three, *Ways in Which Teachers May Incorporate the Cultural and Social Contributions of Family into Schools,* by Ellen Chernoff, SETRC Leader, describes the importance of celebrating cultural differences as we prepare teachers for diverse classrooms. She suggests numerous models and gives supporting research to encourage educators to try these strategies. Her suggestions clearly give educators specific ideas related to incorporating the cultural and social contributions of families and communities in schools. The arts are not forgotten and the author assures us that they are essential for all people.

Section Four, *Activities to Empower Parents as Collaborators in Their Children's Education*, by Amanda Fenlon, Assistant Professor of Education at SUNY Oswego, clearly describes the many activities that empower families as collaborators in their children's education. Her work is supported with research and promotes bringing families into the education process to listen and learn rather than assigning and telling what should be done. This is a gentle chapter with many logical and positive ideas.

Section Five, *Positive Leadership For Family Engagement*, by Peter Kozik, Syracuse University doctoral student and school administrator, is a gem for all compassionate educators. He has contributed an unforgettable case study to set the stage for specific research-based actions. School leadership can make or break a school, so an administrator who understands the importance of effective communication as well as setting the stage for family and community involvement can make a real difference in all of the schoolchildren's academic and social achievement.

The *Afterword*, written by Patricia Ruggiano Schmidt, Le Moyne College Literacy Professor, summarizes the document and provides the reader with a brief overview of research and practice related to culturally relevant pedagogy. She explains that this way of teaching actually stimulates home–school–community connections, naturally. She sees teachers who implement culturally relevant pedagogy as change agents who recognize and make use of family and community funds of knowledge for their students emotional, social, and academic growth and development. Furthermore, she alerts us to the valuable *Appendices* at the end of the document. These are additional resources and ideas for schools to adapt in their quest for an appropriate family engagement framework.

Last, but certainly not least, the two designated parent partners on our team, Diane Heller and Mary Beth Schillace, were consultants, discussants, readers, and editors for this document. Even though all of the members of the initial study group were parents, we believed that we needed to include additional parents of typical and special needs students who could critically analyze the work of teacher educators. They joined us throughout the process—questioning, suggesting, and praising. They collected books and articles and always reminded us of other perspectives. These two special parents gave us the realities and stories to keep us on track and help us produce a work that we believe is practical, useful, and hopeful.

Specifically, Marybeth Schillace provided us with insights as she allowed us to peer into her world as a parent advocating for her child's abilities and disabilities. Diane Heller, at our last meeting, asked to write the *Epilogue* for this document from the parent perspective. We were pleased with the idea and shocked that we hadn't thought about this sooner. We had overlooked the very people we were supposed to be engaging! We apologized, but then were encouraged with Diane's statement, "But you all inspired us!" Diane also inspired Marybeth to write the second reflection for the *Epilogue.*

So, we leave the reader to enjoy the process of learning from this text. We hope this document validates the work you are already doing for home-school-community engagement and encourages you to try new ideas in this important enterprise of educating our nation's children.

REFERENCES

Boykin, A.W. (1984). Reading achievement and the social-cultural frame of reference of Afro-American children. *Journal of Negro Education, 53*(4), 464–473.

Edwards, P.A. (2004). *Children's literacy development: Making it happen through school, family, and community involvement.* Boston, MA: Allyn & Bacon.

Goldenberg, C.N. (1987). Low-income Hispanic parents' contributions to their first-grade children's word-recognition skills. *Anthropology and Education Quarterly, 18,* 149–179.

Heath, S.B. (1983). *Ways with words: Language life and work in communities and classrooms.* Cambridge, UK: Cambridge University Press.

Ladson-Billings, G. (1994). *The dreamkeepers: Successful teachers of African American children.* San Francisco, CA: Jossey-Bass.

Ladson-Billings, G. (1995). Culturally relevant teaching. *Research Journal, 32*(3), 465–491.

Moll, L.C. (1992). Bilingual classroom studies and community analysis: Recent trends. *Educational Researcher, 21*(2), 20–24.

Shartrand, A.M., Weiss, H.B., Kreider, H.M., & Lopez, M.E. (1997). *New skills for new schools: Preparing teachers in family involvement.* Cambridge, MA: Harvard Family Research Project.

Trueba, H.T., Jacobs, L. & Kirton, E. (1990). *Cultural conflict and adaptation: The case of the Hmong children in American society.* New York: The Falmer Press.

Walker-Dalhouse, D. & Dalhouse, A.D. (2001). Parent-school relations: Communicating more effectively with African American parents. *Young Children,* 75–80.

CHAPTER 1

HOME-TO-SCHOOL COMMUNICATION

Grace Ibanez Friedman
Assistant Professor—St. John's University

> *"All education is a continuous dialogue—questions and answers*
> *that pursue every problem on the horizon."*
>
> —William O. Douglas

While waiting for the conference to begin, Mary's mother noticed a hand-written questionnaire on the teacher's desk. She anticipated that it would be shared with her, but it isn't proffered until she inquires about it. It was written up on her daughter the year before and filled out by another adult familiar with Mary, but not Mary's current caretaker or teacher. Mary's mother felt that she should have been informed that this questionnaire was being shared amongst the staff. The mother informed the teacher that the behavioral interventions are out of the question. In fact, she stated that if these are in

Preparing Educators to Communicate and Connect with Families and Communities, pages 1–18
Copyright © 2005 by Information Age Publishing
All rights of reproduction in any form reserved.

any way implemented, she will call a case conference to have Mary's IEP changed to include visual and oral domains in every objective. The teacher and Mary's mother have had no previous conflicts, and the teacher had no desire to start an antagonistic relationship, especially since Mary will be graduating into a public kindergarten the following year. Both parties quickly dropped the matter, and no further reference was made to either Mary's behavior or any proposed change in her IEP. It was not clear how both parties felt after the meeting, but little changed for Mary.

INTRODUCTION

In our global village, educators must be aware of not only what they say, but also how they say it. We serve so many children from diverse families, it also becomes important to understand that what we say has as much positive impact as how we say it. Awareness of this will increase collaboration among all parties involved in the education of our children: home, school, and community.

Initially, we are not going to speak of typical forms of home-to-school communication; the list is as endless as it is old hat: phone calls, notes sent home, newsletters, handbooks, flyers, websites, Friday homework folders, face-to-face conversations, articles placed in newspapers, newscasts, and official letters. These have their place in our professional tool kit. This is not to say these should be ignored, but that a plethora of how-to articles and books have already flooded the marketplace of ideas. Some examples of these are contained in Appendix A.

Instead, we will examine the dynamics encountered when negotiating for collaborative practice and effective two-way communication. The following case study illustrates how we listen, hear, and interpret an exchange between the home and school.

I heard the above story as a parent told it to a small group of educators and parents. A short time later, the parent responded directly to my write-up of the account. I also visited the school in which the situation took place and spoke with the various teachers and therapists involved. It is an illustration of how differing points-of-view may lead to different understandings, and thus can be the basis of miscommunication and conflict.

Parents, as well as educators, may not always choose words that ensure harmonious relationships. Parents' first concern is always their children's welfare, and any perceived or real threat to that welfare is zealously repelled. Teachers with formal training may underestimate the parents' knowledge of their children, or be unaware of any particularly sensitive points regarding the views parents hold of their children. Thus, unwittingly, teachers may share solutions that the parents may not be ready to hear, let alone implement.

SAME STORY, DIFFERENT POINTS-OF-VIEW

Mary attends an inclusive pre-school setting, selected by her parents over a freestanding pre-school for children with similar disabilities. She was born with Down syndrome, which the parents have accepted from the first day of her life. Both parents are college educated and completely devoted to her care. The parents are religious and receive ample support from the church and surrounding community to best serve Mary's needs. She is the youngest of three children, all of who will be attending local public schools in the coming year.

Since early on, Mary has received the best available early intervention services. Mary signs and speaks to communicate and has no hearing deficiencies that commonly occur with Down syndrome. She speaks in 2–4 word phrases. She has mild difficulties with the use of her opposable thumbs, which is common with children who have her condition. She is petite of build and pretty to the extreme. No one can avoid being taken in by her infectious smile. Her mobility is near normal for four years of age. She is amongst the higher functioning children in a cohort of 15 children with the same disabling condition who were born in the area within the same year. I can attest to her energy level and awareness. She ran, jumped, climbed, sat during circle time and snack time, and used toys appropriately when I visited her pre-school program. The school has a successful history of including other children with special needs. Her school adjustment has been unremarkable to date.

Mary's mother has just completed the course sequence in education after having worked in public relations. During the fall semester, Mary's mother received a call from Mary's special education teacher indicating that Mary was having behavioral problems in school, and the teacher requested that she come in for a parent conference. Mary's mother had studied and read about behavioral approaches and was adamantly against them for her daughter. She feels these approaches would overlook Mary's strengths in the visual and oral domains. Mary's mother's mind is made up before the teacher can state why she feels these approaches might work.

When I e-mailed the mother my account of her story, she wrote back to me. I edited her extensive comments in order to illustrate that the gap between hearing what a speaker said, and what the speaker meant or intended can be quite large.

Hello Grace:

Yes, I run 100 mph! Here are my comments. I hope you don't mind that my feedback is so lengthy.

First thoughts:

Immediately after Mary was born, our thought regarding the statement made to us that she might have Down syndrome, ...remains constant...We kindly asked the medical staff to stop mentioning denial and grief...we refused to be part of a statistic of grievers. It was the medical professionals who were consistently positive that we felt were "on our side." We favored these positive professionals and the great hopes that they sent our way regarding Mary...We held high expectations and hope for Mary as she spent the first 39 days of her life in the hospital's neonatal unit. When we looked at our baby on the day she was born, and as she lay in critical condition, the immediate thoughts that we had were that we were facing a life-or-death situation and that we wanted Mary to live. The fact that Mary might have Down syndrome was not the issue at hand at her birth. It was that we wanted her to live. Mary is our child and we will do all in our power to seek the best for her. Another immediate thought upon Mary's birth was that there would be absolutely no room for individuals who expressed feelings of pity or reservation when it came to being with Mary regardless of the situation.

Second thoughts:

Your perception that my husband and I are deeply religious is true...Maybe religiously rooted is the best way to describe us. I think that mainstream society (I may be totally wrong) might view a person who is termed deeply religious as a person who leaves it all up to God. In our case, we leave things to God, but know that God doesn't help those who don't do some of the work on their own.

(Referring to sign language) Encouraging Mary to use sign language with the spoken word was one of the best decisions that we made to enhance her cognitive development. We knew that she was likely to be delayed in her speech...One of the big debates that I was exposed to when we made our decision to use sign was that teaching sign may encourage Mary to rely only on visual cues and visual sign communication. So, I was firm when I dealt with her speech therapist that the signing must be accompanied by verbal cues. Now when Mary gets stuck on a word, we sign the word and say it. She signs it back and says it. Eventually she drops the sign totally. This was the best way to go!

Mary presently speaks using 2–4 word phrases. This is really good for her age in view of her having Down syndrome. She is not frustrated about communicating her wants/needs with us and those who work with her, and we are not frustrated with trying to understand her. This makes for a good relationship between parties.

(Referring to a comment about the use of thumbs) The way that I have most commonly heard therapists talk about difficulties concerning the use of thumbs due to irregular spacing of thumbs—common in individuals who have Down syndrome—is that they "have difficulty with fine motor skills" when they are learning to use fingers in earlier ages. Mary must practice these skills with her occupational therapist.

Third thoughts:

(Referring to a comment that "Mary's mother has studied…") I am not against behavioral approaches. However, the best way to describe my stance is, "Mary's mother has studied and read about behavioral approaches and is adamantly against them for her daughter if the intention is to use the approaches for her daughter as a first resort. She feels…."

Fourth thoughts:

My emphasis on IEP changes primarily focused on VISUAL. I clarified this to the special education teacher and therapy team by stating that sign with the spoken word and pictures used to stress what was being taught must be used consistently and often.

I believe that your vignette will really get the professionals thinking about a lot relative to how my situation was handled and how it might better be handled in the future. I hope that those who read it will see that I as a parent have much factual information upon which I've based my course of action for Mary. Professionals have much to offer, but they should consider themselves only a part of the picture, and not the whole when it comes to advocacy for any student.

The mother wrote back a second time.

I am not certain how long the special education teacher has taught for, but the special education teacher came to me with recommendations via another strong advocacy mom who has a son who happens to have Down syndrome… Aside from my behavioral clash with the special education teacher, the special education teacher has been an integral part of keeping Mary's therapy team as a tight group and all are in close communication with each other.

Mary's special education teacher, speech therapist, PT and OT try to do their sessions with Mary as Mary engages in activities that the class is doing at the time… Some of the therapies and therapy goals overlap with what the special education teacher focuses on in her sessions. There are times when Mary is pulled out. But generally, we have gradually made it so that almost all therapy sessions are done in the classroom as regular classroom activities are happening. All therapists meet Mary at school. It is my understanding, based on the CSE chairperson's responses to my questions, that Mary is receiving minimal services as compared to students who attend a nearby center that focuses mainly on students with special needs.

To ascertain a fuller picture of the situation, the author visited Mary's pre-school and found it everything the parent described: an ideal inclusive pre-school setting, material-rich with lots of flexibility and acceptance for individuality. The teachers and therapists who were interviewed and observed seemed truly interested in the welfare of all the children. The author was particularly interested in the special educator's view and thus conversed with her at length on-site. The special education teacher, after consideration, withdrew her consent to be directly included in the vignette. According to the mother, the special education teacher later expressed concern that she wasn't aware of any breach in communication until she read a draft copy of the incident. The author honored the special educator's request.

STATEMENT OF EMBEDDED ISSUES

This vignette, in a sense, is a tale that never ends, but will evolve as Mary, her mother and teachers get a better understanding of what works for all parties. However, were we to analyze it as a snapshot in time, it offers some interesting and significant issues to be examined. The vignette is atypical in the sense that the parent isn't naïve or uninformed about her child's entitled access to a free and public education (FAPE). She easily quotes chapter and verse from federal statutes governing children with disabilities. Nonetheless, there is much to be learned from it.

First, the sender and receiver in any given situation may interpret what they say or hear differently. Mary's mother accepted for the most part what I had written, but wanted to clarify specific points so I would understand what she intended to say. We were literally painting different word images from the same word cues. Yet I was under the impression I had gotten the message clearly and was simply summarizing the information in an accurate and concise way.

Second, the sender and receiver may believe that they actually understand each other precisely, but due to their need structure or role may come to different solutions. It is futile to try to convince someone to do something that violates his or her values. This was made apparent when Mary's special education teacher tried to offer a new way of supporting Mary's growth, which conflicted with the mother's sense of what is important.

Third, and not previously stated, I would speculate that some of the mother's reactions were in part due to her levels of personal stress. It is stressful to have to deal with a child with a disability, regardless of how much you love that child. It is stressful to have to negotiate a placement each year for your child. It is also stressful to be out of regular work, as both parents were during the course of the year that the incident took place. The author is uncertain how much of this information the school was aware of, but it is likely that it was a contributing factor. Under stress, we are less likely to listen to ideas for change that may endanger our personal equilibrium. Thus, states of feeling affect listening and speaking.

Fourth, we all have personal narratives, and these will conflict with so called facts, the "Roshamon" phenomena. "Roshamon" is the name of a famous Japanese film in which a murder is depicted from four viewpoints. It has come to symbolize that situations are seen differently, depending on the person's filters. So we must not assume that because we speak a language in common that we are effectively communicating. An examination of one's own belief system is in order to keep us from being egocentric.

Fifth, Mary's mother wants to be consulted when information is shared across grades or by different professionals. In the course of our debriefing, I pointed out that work products such as student reports are commonly shared amongst professionals without necessarily sharing this information with parents. However, parents do have a right to see all that's contained in a child's folder. Teachers need to be sensitive to parental wariness about what is written and included in discussions.

Last, the presenting situation seemed to have worked itself out, but imagine if there had been other factors in play. For example, what if the relationship between the mother and special education teacher had not been long-term and based on trust? What if there were differences of language, class, ethnicity, or education between the mother and special education teacher? What if there was a rushed meeting to come to quick closure? The likelihood is that miscommunication and conflict would be more likely to occur if these or other factors were in play.

CONSIDERATIONS IN BUILDING GOOD HOME–SCHOOL COMMUNICATION

The vignette above opens a close-up view of a single situation, but in order to better understand communication, a broader understanding is necessary. Communication is a complex topic. One author refers to five elements in the process: the source of information; the encoder of the message; the channel or medium; the decoder of the message; and the receiver's action or feedback (Bagin, 2001). Any missteps or changes along this process result in miscommunication. Berger (2004) points out the following: the message is affected by the words used, the body language of the participants, and the vocal characteristics of the message (pitch, loudness, speed). Barriers are not limited to the above, as the use of educational jargon, ambiguous language, and the affective state of the speakers may decrease effective communication. Parents, as well as the school and teachers, can put up barriers. Barriers are reduced when both parties actively listen, show honest respect for the other, and communicate regularly.

The following thoughts were taken from the literature on parent involvement and provide ideas on ways to improve communication. The list is not all-inclusive but illustrative of what may influence communication with parents, especially those families with children with special needs. The list is not intended to give a weighting of importance to any particular factor; it is simply to make the reader aware of factors in home-school communication.

Communication and the learning team (Berger)

Teachers, parents, and students are members of the learning team— they share common goals, allowing each student to achieve at the optimum level. Parents should occupy 50% or more of the verbal space. Communication is most effective when it is open, non-ambiguous, reflective, and non-judgmental. Parent-teacher, and parent-teacher-child meetings are opportunities to develop a "team" approach to learning.

Feedback and two-way communication (Bagin)

Feedback, face-to-face, and two-way communication have the most immediate and influential effect on persuasion and decision making. Schools are more effective when there is a parent-school relationship. Special interest groups—senior citizens, grandparent caretakers, single parents, and key communicators within and without these groups—regulate the relationship. Key communicators control the flow of information to and from the school. Critics may have a specific agenda, or lack the emotional stability or knowledge base to make informed judgments. Some critics will be satisfied when they are given clear directives. Others cannot be convinced, but the goal is to understand their point of view.

Special populations (Bagin)

Multiethnic subgroups should be treated in a culturally sensitive manner. Individuals should have the ability to communicate orally, and by written announcement, in the subgroups' native languages. Face-to-face meetings will lessen the dangers of misinterpretation.

School services and special events (Bagin)

The telephone is a key contact point with the community. Voice mail should not be the first contact a parent has with the school. A live person should answer the call initially and then, if necessary, transfer the call to a specific person's mailbox or voice mail.

Communication styles (Bush)

When we communicate with others, we select from a range of behavioral styles: passive, aggressive, passive-aggressive, and assertive. Each style is characterized by an appraisal of who has the power. For example, in the passive style the sender is communicating that the receiver is OK, but not the sender. In the other styles, variations on this theme are sent: I am OK, but you are not; I am OK, and you are not, but I won't let you know I know this about you; and finally I am OK and you are OK. We vary these styles according to a situation, so no one type is inherent. Sometimes the choice is automatic, other times chosen.

Every Person Influences Children (EPIC) has identified communication styles in a different way: (1) Distractor—uses energy warding off confrontation by distracting with unrelated questions or statements; (2) Calculator—avoids talking on the feeling level; intimidates others by constantly citing "facts;" (3) Accuser—makes people feel helpless and angry; (4) Communicator—uses honest and direct language to say what is needed or wanted.

Roadblocks to communication (Berger)

Parents sometimes assume roles which block communication: protector; an "inadequate me" posture; an avoidance of school events; or a club-waving advocate. Schools also pose roadblocks: they ignore the parent as a partner; pass the buck; protect the school turf; or pretend to be too busy to attend to parents. Thus, miscommunication can be a two-way process.

Parent-teacher communication: who's talking? (Fuller & Olsen)

Successful parent-teacher collaborations are designed; they do not happen by accident. Establishing a working, co-equal relationship between teacher and parent is dependent on building trust and open, non-judgmental communications. Feedback from teacher to parent should be specific to that parent's child: bring samples of work, point out pluses and minuses, and formulate a strategy. Using education jargon leads to misunderstandings and ambiguity, which are trustbusters. And finally, parent-teacher communication is one between equals (partners), rather than a lecture from the informed to the uninformed.

Communication techniques (Gestwicki)

Parent–teacher interactions enhance parents' involvement in their children's lives and education. Opportunities to talk/communicate include: child drop-off and pick-up, telephone calls, personal notes, bulletin boards, newsletters, daily newsflash, and suggestion box.

Parent–teacher conferences (Gestwicki)

Parent–teacher conferences are an opportunity for parents and teachers to share information (find out pieces of the puzzle) and identify areas of strength and mutual concerns. Important variables include the following:

- Arrange to have a quiet, private meeting place;
- Establish positive rapport;
- Create good eye contact and show respect for the parents' knowledge and understanding of their child;
- Make non-judgmental, behaviorally oriented observations; and
- Summarize important points of the conference, and agree on subsequent behaviors to be monitored or initiated.

Two-way communications during conferences (Swap)

Conferences present unique challenges to parents and teachers. Of critical importance is the need for individual conferences that highlight the unique characteristics of each child. If parents suspect that the teacher lacks understanding of the unique characteristics of their child, they will dismiss other important information. Conferences need to be two-way communications or there will be no "alliance" with the parent.

Written communication (Diffily)

Teachers and administrators communicate with the families of their students. Teachers' messages will communicate information specific to their grades, classes, and individual students. Administrators will communicate about the general policies, procedures, rules, and incidents that affect the entire school-community family.

Father involvement in early childhood programs (Fagan)

Father involvement in early childhood educational experiences is influenced by the attitudes towards fathers expressed by the school, and by their female partners' attitudes about their parenting skills. Fathers indicated that their greatest need was information about their children's special needs, followed by information on how they could help in their children's programs. Programs can support father involvement with one-way mirrors, direct communication, observation, attendance at conferences, and by daily or weekly newsletters detailing work/play that involves their children. Creating a father-friendly environment sends a strong message to fathers that their input is necessary and important to their children's overall progress.

Contemporary families (Diss & Buckley)

By 1978, the typical American family changed from a nuclear family with working father, stay-at-home mother, and two children to today's families where no single definition of family suffices. Families may be created by blood ties, marriage, or adoption. Today, a teacher must be prepared to relate to students from a variety of family structures: intact, blended, single parent and non-traditional families headed by foster parents, grandparents, and same-gendered parents. Understanding these different families underlies service delivery to students and better home-school communication.

FIVE SUGGESTED MODELS AND EXEMPLARY PROGRAMS TO DEVELOP COMMUNICATION

Fortunately, parent involvement research has been evolving as families change, and we can refer to different models and programs to gather ideas as we develop our own. The following are highlighted summaries of more complex ideas. The reader is urged to further explore the following five suggested models and programs in order to learn more about these strategies.

1. Susanne Carter's Eight Strategy Model for Parental Engagement

Consortium for Appropriate Dispute Resolution in Special Education (CADRE) commissioned Carter to create a scholarly-based framework to enhance parental engagement. These eight factors include the following: family-friendly environment; supportive infra-structure; family-friendly communication; support for family on the home front; educational opportunities for families; home, school, and community partnerships; and the preparation of educators to deal with the home, school, and community. Carter also identifies five schools or districts that implement good communication programs.

Contact information:

CADRE
P.O. Box 51360 (Mailing Address)
Eugene, Oregon 97405-0906
3411-A Willamette Street (Location)
Eugene, Oregon 97405-5122
www.directionservice.org/cadre
Phone: (541) 686-5060
Fax:(541) 686-5063

2. James Comer's School Development Model

Comer, world-renowned child psychiatrist, established a center at Yale to study and develop school and home partnerships. The center has assisted thousands of schools across the nation to include parents in all aspects of school culture: governance, curriculum, instruction, assessment, and guidance. He premised the work of the center on his own family's successful rise from poverty into material success and professional achievement due to strong parental support. His seminal work, *Maggie's Dream,* tells the story of the hard work his parents put into their children's education. All eight siblings became professionals.

Contact information:

> Comer School Development Model
> 55 College Street
> New Haven, CT 06510
> www.info.med.yale.edu/comer
> Phone: (203) 737-1020
> Fax: (203) 737-1023

3. Joyce Epstein's Framework of Parent Engagement

Epstein, famed educational sociologist at Johns Hopkins, has studied the many ways schools engage parents and families. She has developed a six-part framework that is widely referred to or adopted by such organizations as the National PTA. The framework is not a typology, thus no single factor is singled out as better than the next. It identifies six factors and their benefits for children, schools, and families: parenting information, volunteerism, home-school communication, school help for families, parent involvement in school governance, and collaboration with the community.

Contact information:

> Joyce Epstein, Director
> Center on School, Family, and Community Partnerships/CRESPAR
> Johns Hopkins University
> 3003 N. Charles St. Suite 200
> Baltimore, MD 21218
> E-mail: Jepstein@inet.ws.gov
> *www.scov.csos.jhu.edu/p2000/center.htm*
> Phone: (410) 516-8818
> Fax: (401) 516-8890

4. Flora Rodriguez Brown's Project FLAME

Rodriguez Brown and her colleagues at the University of Illinois at Chicago have developed a model for parent involvement designed to improve the simultaneous literacy achievement of parents and children. It was especially designed for Latino families. The model has four key components: developing a home literacy center; parental exposure to literacy models; home literacy instruction; and building home-school relationships by opening communication between families and schools.

Contact information:

> Flora Rodriguez Brown Center for Literacy
> College of Education (M/C 147)
> University of Illinois at Chicago
> 1040 W. Harrison
> Box 4348
> Chicago, Illinois 60680
> *www.uic.edu/educ/flame/contactflame.html*
> E-mail: florab@uic.edu
> Phone: (312) 996-3013
> Fax: (312) 355-2472

5. Patricia Ruggiano Schmidt's ABC's of Communication

Ruggiano Schmidt, literacy professor at Le Moyne College, uncovered the obstacles posed by not being cognizant of underlying cultural and linguistic differences between the home and school. She has developed a teacher training model to inform and prepare teachers to better serve their diverse communities. This model consists of an autobiographical exploration of one's belief systems and early education; a biography of another from a different cultural background; a cross-cultural analysis; and steps to take for parents and teachers to enhance communication based on prior actions.

Contact information:

> Patricia Ruggiano Schmidt
> Le Moyne College
> Education Department
> 101 Reilly Hall
> Syracuse. NY 13214-1399
> Schmidt@lemoyne.edu
> Phone: (315) 445-4793
> Fax: (315) 445-4744

CONCLUSION

We have presented quite an array of issues and factors to consider with respect to home-school communication. Mary's vignette is unusual in its completeness and the access to the persons involved. We recognize it is not typical, yet it contains some universal issues to ponder. We don't expect that all issues will be relevant to your situation, but that there is enough to give you something to think about, and something to act upon.

The good news is that there are good and better ways to develop home-school communication. We invite you to review the points taken from the literature and the five models as you select and design your own approach to effective parent communication.

The bad news is that there is no canned process, where one selects a single textbook and follows it like a cookbook. This is not unfamiliar to teachers, new and experienced. We are experts at modifying materials developed for others. We hoped in this section to alert you to issues in the development of effective communication strategies and tools. You can review Appendix A for checklists that may help to guide your home–school efforts.

Teachers are the first and foremost contact parents have with the schools. It is incumbent that they be the best communicators they can possibly be. They also have the shared responsibility (administrators carry the weight as well) to inform parents of their rights within the law, as time-consuming and cumbersome as that may be. Otherwise, two-way communication is compromised, if not made impossible, rendering "parents as partners" an empty slogan.

Keeping in mind that 6,000 languages exist worldwide, thus 6,000 multiplied by billions of persons with whom to interact and communicate also exist. We all hope to achieve communication but need to appreciate that it is not an automatic conclusion. We hope the remaining sections elucidate other equally important factors: competing spheres of influence, collaborative relationships, socio-linguistic factors, and how administrators can support teachers to be better home-school communicators and collaborators.

REFERENCES

Bagin, D. & Gallagher, D.R. (2001). *The school and the community relations.* Needham Heights, MA: Allyn & Bacon.

Berger, E.H. (2004). *Parents as partners in education: Families and schools working together.* Upper Saddle River, NJ: Pearson Education, Inc.

Berns, R. (2004). *Child, family, school community: Socialization and support.* Belmont, CA: Wadsworth/Thomson Learning.

Bigner, J.J. (2002). *Parent-child relations: An introduction to parenting.* Upper Saddle River, NJ: Pearson Education, Inc.

Bush, J. (2001). *Dollars and sense: Planning for profit in your child care business.* Ontario, Canada: Thompson Learning.

Carter, S. (2002). *Educating our children together.* Eugene, Oregon: CADRE.

Comer, J.P. (1985). *Educating poor minority children.* Scientific American off print. Madison Ave, NY: W.H. Freeman & Company.

Comer, J.P. (1986). Parent participation in the schools. *Phi Delta Kappan, 67*(6), 442–446.

Des Jardins, C. (1971). *How to organize an effective parent group and move bureaucracies.* [Brochure]. Chicago: Coordinating Council for Handicapped Children.

Douglas, William O. (Oct. 1956). *Wisdom.*

EPIC Program. (1993). *Growing and learning together: A family involvement and support program for parents of young children*. [Brochure]. Buffalo, NY: Every Person Influences Children, Inc.

EPIC Program. (1996). *Growing up together: Primary grades*. [Brochure]. Buffalo, NY: Every Person Influences Children, Inc.

Epstein, J. (1995). School/family/community partnerships. *Phi Delta Kappan, 76,* 701–712.

Fagan, J. & Palm, G. (2004). *Fathers and early childhood programs*. Clifton Park, NY: Delmar Learning.

Fuller, M.L. & Olsen, G. (1998). *Home-school relations: Working successfully with parents and families*. Needham Heights, MA: Allyn & Bacon.

Garanzini, M.J. (1995). *Child-centered, family sensitive schools: An educator's guide to family dynamics*. Washington, DC: National Catholic Educational Association.

Gestwicki, C. (2000). *Home, school and community relations: A guide to working with families*. Albany, NY: Delmar.

Goetz, K. (Ed.). (1992). *Programs to strengthen families: A resource guide*. Chicago: Family Resource Coalition.

Goldberg, S. (2002). *Constructive parenting*. Boston, MA: Allyn & Bacon.

Gonzalez-Mena, J. (2002). *The child in the family and the community*. Upper Saddle River, NJ: Pearson Education, Inc.

Hamner, T.J. & Turner, P.H. (2001). *Parenting in contemporary society*. Needham Heights, MA: Allyn & Bacon.

Hannigan, I. (1998). *Off to school: A parent's-eye view of the kindergarten year*. Washington, DC: National Association for the Education of Young Children.

Head Start Bureau. (1991). *Comprehensive child development program—A national family support demonstration* (DHHS Publication No. ACF 92-31267). Washington, DC: U.S. Government Printing Office.

National PTA. (1997). National standards for parent/family involvement programs. Chicago, IL.

Oglan, G.R. & Elcombe, A. (2001). *Parent to parent: Our children, their literacy*. Urbana, IL: Whole Language Umbrella; National Council of Teachers of English.

Olsen, G. & Fuller, M.L. (2003). *Home-school relations: Working successfully with parents and families*. Boston, MA: Allyn & Bacon.

Rogoff, B., Turkanis, C.G. & Bartlett, L. (Eds.). (2001). *Learning together*. New York: Oxford University Press.

Schmidt, P.R. (2002). *Cultural conflict and struggle: Literacy learning in a kindergarten program*. New York: Peter Lang.

Schmidt, P.R. (1995). Working and playing with others: Cultural conflict in a kindergarten literacy program. *The Reading Teacher, 48*(5), 404–412.

Swap, S.M. (1993). *Developing home-school partnerships: From concepts to practice*. New York: Teachers College Press.

TEACHER ACTIVITIES

Enhance Two Way Communication

Humans uniquely use language to communicate. We take this incredible skill as a given. But it must be developed in order to reach beyond our immediate circle of people who can read our minds.

Without taking a course or leaving the comfort of your arm chair, you will become a better communicator if you practice the following:

KWL

Know yourself... My colleague Ruggiano-Schmindt has studied how cultural differences may decrease home/school communication. She suggests a three-part strategy called the ABC's of communication. If uncomfortable using it with a parent, first try it with a colleague.

ABC'S OF COMMUNICATION
Getting to Know You in a Few Minutes
(Schmidt, 1998)

Try this strategy with a colleague first. Then you may want to try it with a parent to develop your relationship. Additionally, this strategy helps to build classroom community from the beginning of the school year. It can be completed in about 5–10 minutes. There are five steps; they can begin in small groups and pairs on a daily basis until students have personally shared with all. Similarities and difference can be celebrated every day.

1. **Autobiography**—close your eyes and think about your earliest memories about family, education, religion, happy times...anything that you remember that you can share with another person
2. **Biography**—one person shares for a minute only those memories he or she wishes to share while the other listens. The listener then shares for a minute.
3. **Compare and Contrast**—together they discuss similarities and differences in life experiences.
4. **Describe this brief experience to the rest of the group in a word or a phrase**

Early learners may choose to talk about something they like or some event that has happened with a classmate, while practicing listening, sharing, and reporting to the whole group. The teacher may record similarities and differences each day. The class may read them together and write their own.

- Know how you prefer to communicate. Take a personal inventory: Is face to face your most effective mode, or over the phone or writing? Recognize what you do well, and work on what needs improvement.
- Know how parents prefer receiving information. In some schools word of mouth works better, suggesting a telephone tree and in other schools notes and newsletters. Thus, know your audience! This also changes from parent to parent. Being a good communicator is identifying other's preferences, and meeting them whenever possible.

- What are your goals in communicating: each situation is different. Be clear when it's just a quick social contact, when you are conveying sensitive information, when you are conveying general information. These distinctions matter.
- When you communicate is important. Some information is time sensitive, other information has no expiration date. Act accordingly.
- When and where you communicate is critical. Sensitive information deserves it's own space. Be sure to have privacy and a quiet space to share sensitive information. Be sure that you leave time for the parent to respond, or make a follow up appointment.

- Learn to pace yourself. Pick a style and frequency level that meets your personality. Whether it's once a month, weekly or daily, make sure it's consistent.
- Learn to write simply. Keep jargon and judgmental information from your notes and newsletters home. Have another person read what you have written before you send it out.
- Learn to be patient with the adults. While children are innately programmed to please you, their parents are not. Some of my best experiences with parents resulted from long term contact. Be a turtle, not a hare.

Take the following quiz:

1. Taking time to communicate with parents is a central part of my job:

True				False
5	4	3	2	1

2. When I communicate successfully with parents I feel I have helped the child to do their best as well:

True				False
5	4	3	2	1

3. I can do a better job for the children I teach, when I know more about their family and their parents expectations:

True				False
5	4	3	2	1

4. Establishing trust is a two way street, not a guarantee:

True				False
5	4	3	2	1

5. When I communicate with parents I honor my children and my professional ethics:

True				False
5	4	3	2	1

Score yourself:

Perfect score is 25. Keep going!

Good score is between 15 and 24.

Improvement score is 14 or less.

Whatever your score, keep in mind that we are a profession offering hopeful outcomes. Communication is one tool in our repertoire to keep children motivated to learn, and parents involved enough to support us.

CHAPTER 2

ASCERTAINING AND INFLUENCING PRE-SERVICE TEACHER DISPOSITION(S) TO FAMILY ENGAGEMENT

Tracy Knight Lackey
Assistant Professor—Syracuse University

I went from teaching at an all Black middle school in the South, to teaching at a diverse middle school in the Midwest. It was a culture shock to teach at a school where students were Black, White, Latino, and Asian. Even though I felt like a competent teacher, I went through some changes because the children were different, just different.

(Journal reflection of a novice teacher)

Current concerns regarding the quality of education have urged us to examine and re-examine educational paradigms or schools of thought related to curricular content, as well as the human element involved in teaching and learning. Educational research indicates that effective teachers are those who possess competency in their respective area(s) of specialization. Additionally, it has been established that interpersonal and intrapersonal qualities of teachers also impact student learning and development. Take, for example, the opening vignette: the teacher was pre-

Preparing Educators to Communicate and Connect with Families and Communities, pages 19–29
Copyright © 2005 by Information Age Publishing
19

pared to impart content knowledge, but first she had to explore some relevant and person-centered principles of practice as follows.

- *Self-perception* including confidence in competency; ability to seek and receive professional advice and feedback; commitment to crafting an expansive and evolving standard(s) of professional ethics; willingness to assess and honor personal beliefs of students and families; and the ability to participate in self-regulated and self-directed teaching and learning.
- *Perceptions of others* such as placing value on views held by relevant education stakeholders (e. g., students and families); innovative ways in which to demonstrate respect towards diverse partners in education; willingness to change instruction to ensure that all students meet standards that are meaningful; and promoting opportunities for active involvement of all families.
- *Perspectives on the meaning of teaching* such as the willingness to move beyond academic content and assume broader responsibilities that address the needs of all families, the community, and society at-large.

For many years, education was viewed from a simple give (presentation of information) and take (retention of information) orientation, but present-day schooling is broader and more complex. It is now seen as an instrument for promoting positive social change, fostering civic participation, and creating an equitable pluralistic society. The aforementioned obligations have never been more difficult to fulfill. Take, for example, one of the controversial issues in education circles today: the gap between the student population and the teaching force. By most demographic accounts, one in every three school children is from an ethnic, racial, or linguistic minority group, while the majority of the teaching force continues to consist of middle-class white women (Education Letter, 1988). Oftentimes, this gap results in negative educational experiences and outcomes.

Heward (2000) and other researchers assert that incongruence in interactions between teachers and culturally diverse students, and incompatible home-school expectations can pose major barriers to effective education. Teachers are more inclined to set appropriate goals for, relate to, and provide support for students, their families, and colleagues who are culturally comparable (e. g., race, ethnicity, socioeconomic status, professional orientation) to themselves.

For example, novice teachers educated in liberal institutions of higher education may be more inclined to support school movements/programs that are based on a distribution of power as opposed to those based on hierarchies of power. One rationale for such a tendency may be the systematic implementation of a democratic-oriented pedagogy. In contrast, children tend to value, and families tend to support, culturally relevant activities in which they have a vested interest. For example, some families with limited resources may be wary of activities that involve labor/work/energy and no monetary return such as unpaid internships or service-learning projects. Such long-term and beneficial activities are hard to grasp when individuals are concerned with immediate basic issues of survival, which require solid resources. In sum, effective teaching and learning can only result from multifaceted, cross-environmental, democracy-oriented, individually germane, collaborative efforts (Cochran-Smith, 1995).

It is also worth noting that the numerous changes society has undergone present a significant number of novel dilemmas. Children in schools today have to contend with a growing number of complex societal problems such as global upheaval, drug abuse, deterioration of family structures, and poverty, to name a few (Hodgkinson, 1989; Peng, Wang and Walberg, 1992; Wilson, 1996). Such problems render mastery of academic content alone insufficient in producing well-adjusted and educated individuals. All things considered, contemporary educators must possess a disposition that empowers them to be masters of academic content, lifelong learners, facilitators of knowledge, and agents of social change.

There are many definitions of disposition, which vary among individuals, organizations, and institutions. In the broadest sense, "Disposition is the natural mental and emotional outlook or mood; characteristic attitude...the natural or prevailing aspect of ones' mind as shown in behavior and in relationships with others" (Webster's New Universal Unabridged Dictionary, 1996, p. 568). Despite the large number of definitions, there is a fairly significant consensus that a favorable disposition is chief among exemplary qualities of professionalism. This position is supported by such entities as the National Council for Accreditation of Teacher Education (NCATE, 2001), which defines disposition as:

> The values, commitments and professional ethics that influence behaviors toward students, families, colleagues, and communities and affect student learning, motivation, and development as well as educator's own professional growth. Dispositions are guided by beliefs and attitudes related to values such as caring, fairness, honesty, responsibility, and social justice.

Further, studies have shown that there is a positive correlation between a favorable disposition and effective teaching and cross-environmental collaboration (McLean, Wolery, & Bailey, 2004). A prime example of effective teaching is mastery of classroom organization and content knowledge. This area of competency usually involves a personal and individual commitment to academic excellence. A primary example, and key component, of cross-environmental collaboration is family engagement. This competency is more complicated because it involves working with, listening to, and respecting a range of individuals in order to meet the needs of children.

Family engagement has become a mainstay firmly rooted in teacher preparation programs, school reform, and academic literature. Although the definition varies, scholars generally agree that this practice symbolizes the manner in which education professionals construct, teach, interact with, and advocate for, children and their families. An intricate array of factors mediates the manner in which educators engage children and their families. Such values include, but are not limited to: conflicting personal principles; outdated institutional constraints; ego-driven and pride-driven perspectives; family experiences; and academic training. Given this set of considerations, a number of challenges and questions have emerged in the higher education community. Namely, what are some ways to ascertain and influence pre-service teacher disposition(s) to family engagement? The following strategies and techniques may prove useful to readers.

Establishing a frame of reference and relevance

In order to promote teaching and learning, it is imperative to provide individuals with a detailed explanation of the required skills/goals/objectives and the importance of their role in the overall process for mastery. For example, it would be beneficial to define and/or provide examples of disposition(s) when attempting to ascertain and/or influence pre-service dispositions. One organizational tool known for accomplishing such a task is *"The Five Dispositions of Effective Teachers"* framework initially introduced by A. W. Combs (1994) as five qualities/beliefs of effective teachers as helpers. They include empathy, a positive view of others, a positive view of self, authenticity, and meaningful purpose and vision.

Facing and embracing reality

Education is life, not just preparation for it. Future teachers must be encouraged to participate in activities and thought processes they are likely to encounter in practice, in order for teaching/content knowledge to take on meaning. For example, students should be challenged to produce and share written and/or verbal reflections of real-life experiences that evoke feelings of discomfort and judgment, such as death and dying, sexuality, drug abuse, sexism, and suicide. These conundrums are operative in the world and will be operative in classrooms. One activity that can be used to promote awareness is the W. A. N. T. exercise, which involves researching/ discussing/answering four simple questions on a given topic such as suicide:

- *Who:* Who are the individuals/students most likely to commit suicide (e.g., gay and lesbian teenagers)?

- *Are:* Are any of these individuals in my classroom? Are any of these individuals in the lives/homes/communities of my students?
- *Needs:* What are the needs of these individuals?
- *Teaching:* How can I meet the needs of these individuals in my teaching activities? If I cannot meet these needs, who can?

Risk taking

All people in the world learn and express themselves in different ways. Future educators should be required to explore verbal and non-verbal modes of communication and perception filters (e.g., language, age, and ethnicity) by participating in activities such as requesting clarity, tolerating constructive feedback, and respectfully negotiating misunderstandings. Students also should be openly questioned on the assorted meanings of words, concepts, and experiences different from their own. For example, students were presented with a brief vignette about a family of six (three of whom are children with disabilities) living in poverty, and making a living by boosting. Students were asked the following questions: Could you pronounce the word boosting? Could you spell it? Can you explain it? The responses to the first two questions were overwhelmingly yes while the responses to the third question were overwhelmingly no. The ensuing discussion was on the necessity of deriving an understanding of such things in a respectful and professional manner.

Fostering self-disclosure

The degree of self-disclosure involved in critical discussions of disposition is often accompanied by, at least, a degree of fear, defensiveness, and embarrassment. Self-disclosure is a practice that varies across cultures with respect to comfort level (Sue & Sue, 1990). One strategy for promoting a working comfort level among pre-service educators is the establishment of guidelines for discussions. Examples of such parameters are: (1) listening carefully to all perspectives presented; (2) observing rules of confidentiality; (3) speaking from one's own firsthand experience; (4) avoiding the use of sweeping generalizations; (5) adequate and equitable timing; and (6) a rule of focus on personal learning (Tatum, 1992).

Utilizing tools of constant re-examination

Pre-service teachers are human beings with their own individual histories, experiences, and beliefs. The culmination of these unique individual characteristics renders sporadic activities ineffective when attempting to examine and/or influence an individual's disposition. For the most part, researchers infer that teachers, by nature, will adhere to their beliefs unless they are systematically and consistently challenged (Hartzell, 1999; Freiberg & Driscoll, 2004). Examples of tools for constant re-examination include: (1) crafting and constantly honing a philosophy of teaching; (2) regular chronicling of activities that relate to teaching, learning, and change; (3) joining or establishing support/work groups; and (4) becoming members of professional educational organizations. These tools can be used in isolation or in conjunction with one another. For example, individuals can be required to: (1) craft a philosophy of teaching, and (2) identify at least two professional organizations that have similar missions.

Drawing from manifold modes of scientific research

Although somewhat controversial, the psychodynamic approach is being put forth as a viable measure for assessing teacher dispositions (Mullin, 2003). This orientation is based on the assertion that dispositions can be determined using research tools with a personalogical basis such as personality profiles, psychological tests, and other psycho-perceptual instruments. Two examples of such instruments are the *"Teacher Attitudes Survey"* and the *"Diagnostic Inventory for Selective Prescription on Self-Evaluation."* As with most courses of research, there are points of criticism. Limitations often associated with the psychodynamic approach include questions of reliability, validity, and a lack of effective tools for assuring trustworthiness and fidelity of data.

Modeling desired behaviors

Modeling of a desired behavior is key to promoting learning, transferring, and the generalizing of desired skills. Several models have been developed to illustrate this point. For example, one of the most noted frameworks that promotes caring dispositions consists of the following four levels (Freeman, 1999): (1) experiencing caring, (2) practicing caring, (3) initiating and sustaining caring relationships, and (4) continuing caring reflections and refinements at the academic level. Specific activities for pre-service teachers, to be implemented by teacher educators, can include: (1) the creation of opportunities for interaction outside of the classroom; (2) taking advantage of teachable moments that reveal/illuminate multiple student perspectives/experiences; (3) modeling/encouraging questioning of established beliefs, norms, and trends; and (4) self-disclosure.

Teachers on display

Arguably, the role of the teacher is that of guide and facilitator. Instructors should not be viewed as sole "owners" of incontrovertible knowledge. All students bring a unique way of knowing into the classroom, and they should be required to express such rich differences. For example, students should be encouraged to craft a graphic representation of their personal perceptions of issues around disability and the resultant effects of these in the classroom. Although provided with general guidelines, students should be encouraged to be as creative and controversial as they dare (e. g., screenplays, handcrafted games, and instructional videotapes). Representations should be shared with fellow students and the families (individuals) with whom students work with throughout the year in practicum or respite experiences.

Advancing triangulated sharing

Triangulated (use of multiple sources and/or methods) sharing entails activities and opportunities for individuals to view and explore each other as unique and evolving beings with shared needs, experiences, and emotions. Such activities establish authentic learning communities and safe spaces for critical exploration (Fink, 2003). A few examples include: (1) person-centered introductions, (2) activities that allow for the assignment of personal meaning, and (3) ice-breaker type activities that establish an atmosphere of collective, active participation.

Encouraging intrinsic motivation

Intrinsic motivation tends to foster a greater sense of purpose, persistence, and insight in individuals. Related skills include self-regulation of thoughts, feelings, and actions that are systematically designed to achieve a goal (Zimmerman, 2000). The following are two examples of activities designed to encourage intrinsic motivation (Wlodkowski, 1999): (1) posing a problem whereby an individual must identify strategies to achieve a specific goal in the face of one or more obstacles, and (2) simulating activities by employing learning procedures that include role-playing, exercises, and games that allow individuals to practice and apply learning in contexts that are nurturing and sufficiently realistic.

Edifying voices of experience

Life histories and stories of change are powerful tools of intimate examination. The knowledge of such things personal is the ideal complement to teaching academic content of any kind, affecting change, influencing public opinion, shaping social and political beliefs, and promoting a diverse and pluralistic society. Pre-service educators should continually examine the personal narratives and lived experiences of educators, both novice and seasoned, and of the children and families with which they will be working.

Employing successful examples of similarity

As mentioned before, teachers are more inclined to set appropriate goals, provide support for, and relate to individuals who are culturally equivalent to themselves. When individuals witness people with similar individual constructs (age, gender, ethnicity, class) engage in a designated activity, such as exploring and enhancing personal dispositions, they tend to believe that they, too, can master such an activity or skill. For example, pre-service teachers can glean a plethora of pertinent and realistic advice from first-year teachers of similar backgrounds who have experienced changes in dispositions towards teaching and/or family engagement.

CONCLUSION

Dispositions are continually being publicized as important dimensions of effective teaching and learning. The difficulty lies in defining and influencing such an idiosyncratic, intrinsically ingrained, and moderated concept (Ritchhart, R. 2002; Smith, Hofer, Gillespie, Solomon & Rowe, 2003). Though a daunting task, it is crucial to promote and explore the plethora of challenges regarding pre-service teacher dispositions if this concept does indeed influence and determine an individual's innate manner of thinking and behaving. It is highly unlikely that dispositions can be influenced by force, but rather by careful design of nurturing environments, exercises, and activities that require pre-service teachers to broaden and modify perspectives, behaviors, and responsibilities in light of new knowledge (Beckman, 1996). For the sake of developing children and effective teaching and learning, education professionals would do well to operate under the assumption that change is always a possibility, even within themselves. As for the teacher involved in the opening vignette, she took the most important steps in becoming a culturally responsive educator by developing self-awareness through exploration, immersion, and discourse about and with her students and their families and by dedicating herself to becoming a lifelong learner. I have never regretted those decisions.

REFERENCES

Beckman, P. (1996). *Strategies for working with families of young children.* College Park, Maryland: Brooks Publishing.

Cochran-Smith, M. (1999). Educational leadership and social justice. *Journal of Leadership in Education, 2.*

Combs, A.W. (1999). *Being and becoming: A field approach to psychology.* New York: Springer Publishing Company Inc.

Dewey, J. (1904). The relation of theory to practice in education. In C.A. McMurry (Ed.), *The relation of theory to practice in the education of teachers.* Third Yearbook of the National Society for the Scientific Study of Education Part I. Chicago, IL: University Press of Chicago.

Cultural differences in the classroom. (1988). *Education Letter, 4,* 1–4.

Fink, D.L. (2003). *Creating significant learning experiences: An integrated approach to designing college courses.* San Francisco, CA: Jossey-Bass.

Freeman, N., Swick, K. & Brown, M. (1999). A caring curriculum within early childhood teacher education programs. *Education, 120,* 161–167.

Freiberg, H.J. & Driscoll, A. (2004). *Universal teaching strategies.* Boston, MA: Allyn & Bacon.

Heward, W. (2000). *Exceptional children: An introduction to special education.* Upper Saddle River, NJ: Prentice Hall.

Hartzell, G. (1999). Indirect advocacy. *Book Report, 18,* 8–11.

Hodgkinson, H.L. (1989). *The same client: The demographics of education and service delivery systems.* Washington, DC: Institute for Educational Leadership.

McLean, M., Wolery, M., & Bailey, B. (2004). *Assessing infants and preschoolers with special needs.* Upper Saddle River, NJ: Prentice Hall.

Mullin, D. (2003). *Developing a framework for the assessment teacher candidate dispositions.* College of Saint Benedict: Saint John's University.

NCATE. (2001). *Standards for professional development schools.* National Council for Accreditation of Teacher Education.

Peng, S.S., Wang, M.C., & Walberg, H.J. (1992). Demographic disparities in inner city eighth graders. *Urban Education, 26,* 441–459.

Ritchhart, R. (2002). *Intellectual character.* San Francisco, CA: Jossey-Bass.

Smith, C., Hofer, J., Gillespie, M., Solomon, M., & Rowe, K. (2003). *How teachers change: A case study of professional development in adult education.* Cambridge, MA: National Center for the Study of Adult Learning and Literacy.

Sue, D.W. and Sue, D. (1990). *Counseling the culturally different: Theory and practice.* New York: Wiley Publishing Company.

Webster's New Universal Unabridged Dictionary. (1996). p. 568.

Wilson, W.J. (1996). *When work disappears.* USA: Alfred Knoph.

Wlodkowski, R.J. (1999). *Enhancing adult motivation to learn: A comprehensive guide to teaching all adults.* San Francisco, CA: Jossey-Bass.

Zimmerman, B.J. (2000). Attaining self-regulation: A social cognitive perspective. In M. Boekaerts, P. Pintrich & M. Seider (Eds.), *Self-regulation: Theory, research and applications.* Orlando, Florida: Academic Press.

ONLINE RESOURCES

Association for Supervision and Curriculum Development
www.ascd.org

Code of Ethics and Standards of Practice for Educators of Persons with Exceptionalities
www.cec.sped.org/ps/code.html#1

Dispositions of Effective Teacher Survey
education.lamar.edu/PreAdmission/effective_teachers.asp

Fifty Imperatives for Teacher Education 50 Years Post Brown v. Board of Education
www.urbannetworks.net/Documents/imperatives.pdf

National Council for Accreditation of Teacher Education
www.ncate.org

National Network for the Study of Educator Dispositions
www.education.eku.edu/Dean/nnsed.htm

RELEVANT AND INTERESTING READS

Stories of the Courage to Teach: Honoring the Teacher's Heart, Sam Intrator and Parker Palmer, Authors
The Courage to Teach: A Guide for Reflection and Renewal, Rachel Livsey and Parker Palmer, Authors
The First Year of Teaching: Real World Stories from America's Teachers, Pearl Rock Kane, Editor
The Gift of Fire, Richard Mitchell, Author
Teaching, Leading and Learning: Becoming Caring Professionals, Rita A. Jensen and Therese J. Kiley, Authors

TEACHER ACTIVITIES

1. Identify, observe, and interview a teacher who has a strong sense of connection to a local school and the surrounding community. The interview questions should spur a discussion of views on the role of dispositions in teaching, changes that occurred in dispositions, and factors that promoted or precluded the changes.

2. Conduct a search of professional literature for data/articles on teacher dispositions (present and future teachers). Use the research to inform the crafting of a personal definition of disposition. Discuss it in terms of what it means to teachers.

3. What if you had to inform your fellow students on positive and negative dispositions associated with teaching? Write the script, set the scene, and demonstrate a scenario.

4. Read a narrative (i.e., first hand reflection or case study) concerning teacher dispositions relative to working with families. Highlight any perspectives, experiences, and/or practices that evoke feelings such as consternation, anger or confusion. Why do you think you are

experiencing these emotions? What are the underlying issues? How will they affect your practice?

5. After conducting the initial visit to your practicum or placement, write a letter to yourself documenting your first impression(s) of the school, class, and students. Revisit the document at the middle of the term or conclusion of the placement. Note changes you would make based upon your exposure and experience (i.e., erroneous assumptions, valid predictions, reinforced beliefs).

6. Recall your experience with past teachers; select an example of one with a positive disposition and one with a negative disposition. Compare and contrast the examples. What values, behaviors, and attitudes distinguish the two individuals? To what extent do your observations correspond to data presented in research?

7. Examine a potentially complex situation that might present itself when you begin practice (i.e., angry parent, student living in a same-sex parent household, or student living with HIV/AIDS). Specify the professional and personal knowledge and skills needed to negotiate the state of affairs. How could you be proactive in preparing to encounter such situations and garner necessary competencies?

CHAPTER 3

WAYS IN WHICH TEACHERS MAY INCORPORATE THE CULTURAL AND SOCIAL CONTRIBUTIONS OF FAMILY INTO SCHOOLS

Ellen Chernoff
Teacher In-service Staff Development
Capital Region BOCES

Affirming the right of all human beings to education is to take on a far greater responsibility than simply to assure to each one reading, writing, and arithmetic capabilities; it is to guarantee fairly to each child the entire development of his mental faculties and the acquisition of knowledge and of ethnical values corresponding to the exercise of these faculties until adaptation

Preparing Educators to Communicate and Connect with Families and Communities, pages 31–45
Copyright © 2005 by Information Age Publishing
All rights of reproduction in any form reserved.

to actual social. Moreover, it is to assume the obligation—keeping in mind the aptitudes and constitution that each person possesses—of not destroying or spoiling those possibilities that he may have that would benefit society first of all, or of allowing the loss of important abilities, or the smothering of others. (Piaget, 1973, p. 54)

Not learning tends to take place when someone has to deal with unavoidable challenges to her or his integrity and identity. In such situations there are forced choices and no apparent middle ground. To agree to learn from a stranger who does not respect your integrity causes a major loss of self. The only alternative is not learn and reject their world. (Kohl, 1995, p. 6)

Students who are culturally and linguistically diverse are especially at risk in relation to disability status because most schools are not well prepared to deal with differences in learning, behavior, culture, and language, either separately or in combination...They may be viewed as culturally and linguistically inferior as well as academically and socially incapable due to their disabling condition. (Castellano, 1997, p. 13)

I will always remember the day one of my second-grade students, Alejandro, looked up at me and asked, "Mrs. Bode, are you Latina—are you Puerto Rican?" I smiled and answered, "No, Alejandro, I am Irish-American." He replied, "Why do you love Latino art so much?" "I love it because I learn so much from it. I love so many kinds of art, but you are right, I sure do love Latino art, especially, Puerto Rican Art." As an Irish-American teacher in a classroom with many diverse youngsters, I make a deliberate effort to practice culturally congruent pedagogy. (Bode, 2003, p. 85)

INTRODUCTION AND RATIONALE

Student populations in our schools are becoming increasingly culturally and linguistically diverse (CLD). As reported in USA TODAY (July 2, 2003), four out of ten students belong to a minority group. One out of every five students speaks a language other than English.

Schools and teachers frequently have difficulty meeting the challenge of reaching and teaching CLD learners. Evidence of this is seen in the existence of an achievement gap based on race, higher dropout rates for students of color, and the over-representation of minority students in special education.

Sadly, schools and teachers often fail to recognize and develop the linguistic and cultural skills of CLD students and the possible contribution these skills could bring to the society at large (a la Piaget). Frequently, children from homes where the language is other than English are implicitly (or explicitly) asked to "smother" the home language. This occurs even though these skills would benefit the individual and the larger society.

There are also children who come to school speaking English, but from cultural backgrounds that differ from the majority culture. When schools fail to respect children who are culturally, linguistically, and historically different from the majority, children may experience a "disconnect" between school and home. Given such a choice, some children reject the school culture and engage in what Herbert Kohl calls "willed not learning." In all, there is a "loss of important abilities" which is destructive both to the individual and to society as a whole (p.6).

Piaget (1973) originally wrote *To Understand Is To Invent: The Future of Education*, at the request of the United Nations following World War II. Piaget writes of the acquisition of "ethnical values" in conjunction with the "development of mental faculties and the acquisition of knowledge" (p.54). Undoubtedly, Germany was considered to be a scientifically advanced, highly cultured, and literate society. However, this did not prevent the German nation from adopting policies leading to the death of citizens from many countries in an attempt to exterminate people who were not of Aryan race and culture.

So, for all children, it is not enough for educators and educational systems to develop a discrete set of academic skills. Rather, education is about creating partnerships with families and communities so that our children reach their full social, artistic, linguistic, academic, and intellectual potential, while acquiring the cultural competencies needed to live in a multicultural society. McCaleb (1994), in her book on building communities of learners, writes: 'The students' cultural diversity and the families' lived experience need to become part of the school, *but most importantly, they must become part of the classroom learning environment, and the development of the curriculum.*" [italics added]. (p. 193)

STRATEGIES FOR INCORPORATING CULTURAL AND SOCIAL CONTRIBUTIONS OF FAMILIES

How can teachers incorporate the cultural and social contributions of family into curriculum and instruction? Five strategies are offered as follows.

Providing Culturally Responsive Instruction

Culturally competent teachers are cognizant of cultural diversity in their classrooms. They make sure that the content (curriculum and materials) and the learning activities (instruction) take into account the students' cultures and how culture impacts on learning (learning styles). Montgomery (2001) defines culturally responsive classrooms: "Culturally responsive classrooms specifically acknowledge the presence of culturally diverse students and the need for these students to find relevant connections among themselves and with the subject matter and the tasks the teachers ask them to perform." (p. 4)

Some examples of the use of culturally responsive instruction are as follows.

- *Social Studies Resource Guide With Core Curriculum* (New York State Education Department). Grade 3: Communities Around the World—Learning About People and Places.
  - "People in world communities use legends, folktales, oral histories, biographies, autobiographies, and historical narratives to transmit values, ideas, beliefs, and traditions." (p. 25)
  - "All people in world communities need to learn and they learn in different ways." (p. 25)

- *English Language Arts Resource Guide With Core Curriculum* (New York State Education Department). Standard 2: "Students will read, write, listen and speak for literary response and expression." (Grades 2–4, p. 21).
  - What students listen to: stories; poems and songs; folktales and fables; plays; films and video productions.
  - What students do: (1) compare imaginative texts and performances to personal experiences and prior knowledge; and (2) explain cultural and ethnic features in imaginative texts.

Using the State's core curriculums in English Language Arts and Social Studies, teachers who are culturally competent can:

- Ask students and/or parents to share stories, songs, and rhymes from the home culture.
- Publish and share autobiographies and biographies from students and parents as described in 4b and 4c of this section.
- Read and respond to biographies or people from various cultures and compare them to the biographies of students and parents. Good resources include: *Honoring Our Ancestors: Stories and Pictures by Fourteen Artists* (Rohmer, 1999) and *Just Like Me: Stories and Self-Portraits by Fourteen Artists*, (Rohmer, 1997), both edited by Harriet Rohmer and published by Children's Book Press.
- Select a folktale/folktales that reflect the ethnic and cultural make-up of the classroom and design instructional activities that align with the curriculum, such as the following.

At the end of the Taino folktale, we learn that the people of Puerto Rico made Niguayona a leader. Why do you think he was chosen? What qualities did the Taino people value?

- Working with a partner, make a list of actions from the story that show he would make a good leader.
- Make a poster that shows the qualities of Niguayona that make him a good leader.
- Do you think Niguayona was a good leader? Why or why not? Explain your answer in a paragraph.
- Pretend that you are Atariba and write/draw a thank you card for Niguayona. Be sure to tell Niguayona what makes him a wonderful friend in your message.

Researching Cultures—Teachers as Cultural Researchers

Culturally competent teachers know about or seek information on the home cultures of their students. In order to design classroom activities that correspond to the students' needs, teachers need to know about the values and practices embraced in the students' home cultures. Teachers must also know how cultural values and practices impact upon learning style.

Teachers may read "culture grams" or generalized information about a particular culture or ethnic group. However, the authors of *The Diversity Kit* (developed by LAB at Brown University, 2002) caution that relying on this approach alone can lead to stereotyping. These authors suggest that teachers can gather information about students' home cultures through home visits, conversations with community members, consultations with other teachers, and observations of students in and out of school. Some teachers already engage in these activities and simply need to be more conscious of culture as they do so.

When teachers create classroom activities and assignments, they need to keep cultural values and practices in mind. The following example highlights this important point. In a middle school, students were asked to comment on how their parents handled a particular situation and what they wish their parents had done differently. In addition, one teacher asked the parents to respond to their child's suggestions and indicate how this might influence future interactions.

For some parents and students, this activity would be fine. For others, it would be too personal or intrusive. But for some students and parents, this exercise would be culturally offensive, particularly in traditional Asian cultures. Some cultures do not emphasize explicit verbal expression. In addition, in various cultures it is highly inappropriate for children to comment on their parents' words and actions in a critical way.

Perhaps the goal of the activity was to have the students write a persuasive essay or make a convincing speech. In this case, the activity could be modified as follows.

Think of something you want to do that requires parental permission.
You can:

- Write a letter to your parents to convince them to give you the okay;
- Write a persuasive essay which explains how you would convince your parents;
- Act out the scene with a classmate in the parental role.

Supporting the Home Language

Culturally competent educators value and support the students' home languages. Atunez (2004) cites numerous studies that demonstrate a strong positive correlation between children's native language proficiency and English. Children who have the opportunity to develop their first language (L1) are ultimately more successful in the second language (L2) English (Thomas and Collier, 1997).

The National Association for the Education of Young Children (NAEYC, 1996), in making recommendations for programs and practice, states that educators need to view bilingualism as an asset, and they can help children maintain the home language while developing English language proficiency. NAEYC reports that literacy skills in the home language will be transferred to English. When the teacher speaks the child's home language, NAEYC recommends use of that language in the learning environment with the child such as through the use of charts and books, and throughout the instructional setting such as in the library corner. When the teacher does not speak the child's language, NAEYC suggests the teacher can still affirm the child's language by learning some words, providing a bilingual bulletin board for parents (with help from colleagues), and by having books in the home language available. Teachers can also invite native language speakers to read to the child.

For older students, opportunities to develop cognitively and linguistically in the home language while acquiring English continue to be important. Moran, C. and Tinajero et. al, (1993) point out the increased necessity to motivate older students. Classroom environments that include the students' heritage and language can be motivating. Even when literacy instruction is conducted primarily in English, Freeman, Freeman, and Mercuri (2003) suggest that students be encouraged to "connect their reading and writing in English to their own cultural backgrounds and to value the literacy of their communities including oral literacy traditions." (p. 9)

...when the language and culture of the home are not congruent, teachers and parents must work together to help children strengthen and preserve their home language while acquiring skills needed to participate in the shared culture of the school...Teachers need to respect the child's home language and culture and use it as a base on which to build and extend children's language and literacy. (NAEYC, 1998, p. 39)

Instructional Activities and Curriculum That Incorporate Students' Cultures

Culturally competent educators truly value the funds of knowledge and skills that students acquire at home, and develop curriculum and instruction that incorporate what students have learned from family and community.

Tapping hidden family and community resources

Louis Moll, a researcher and professor at the University of Arizona, believes that teachers can boost the literacy skills and academic achievement of minority students by tapping into the "hidden" home and community resources (North Central Regional Educational Laboratory, 1994). Working with a research team and classroom teachers, Moll and his collaborators developed instructional strategies to tap into the "hidden" resources. Through their investigations in the Tucson area, the team learned that Latino families knew about agriculture, mining, medical folk remedies, carpentry, masonry, and electrical wiring among other areas of expertise.

One sixth-grade teacher who wanted to improve her students' writing skills decided to depart from her traditional instructional approaches. Although she knew nothing about it, this teacher developed a thematic unit on construction. Parents and community members were invited to share their expertise including use of tools and measurement. Students were directed to research and build models. They also wrote short essays in English or Spanish explaining their work. Eventually, the project expanded and the students constructed a model community. The project required the students to report on their research, orally and in writing. By the end of the semester, more than 20 adults had visited the classroom, and the students had done extensive reading and writing. Moll believes that this kind of approach will create a real desire for literacy and a broader (school-parent-community) learning community.

Parents as partners and authors

In *Building Communities and Learners*, Sudia Palomo McCaleb (1994) describes working with a classroom teacher to develop "authors in the classroom." She describes how books were created by first-grade students and their parents and became part of classroom reading materials. The books were based on real-life experiences of the children and their parents. The books celebrate and validate home culture while highlighting family concerns and hopes for the future. Five general content areas were identified, as follows:

- Childhood friendships;
- Families building together;
- Families as problem-solvers through struggle and change;
- Families as protagonists of their own stories; and
- Codification based on community life.

However, McCaleb did not begin with writing books. She became familiar with families by inviting parents to participate in dialogues. She recorded the dialogues, which were later transcribed and printed. McCaleb wanted to gain information about: the parents' own educational experiences; how parents viewed their children's educational experience with the total environment (school, family, and community); and how to create links between the home and school which honor and validate the home culture and community.

Some of the questions included in the dialogues are:

> "Talk about the oral traditions in your family or community (songs, stories, chants, and sayings)."
> "In what ways do you feel that you teach your children? What and how do they teach you?"
> "Talk about the ways in which the school reflects or negates what you teach your children at home." (McCaleb, 1994, pp. 64–65)

Publishing the dialogues allowed parents to see themselves as authors with valuable ideas. It gave McCaleb information about the families, which shaped the subsequent creation of books based on real-life histories and values. By writing and then reading the books, the teacher and the parents became partners for literacy.

Using biography and autobiography to make connections

Schmidt (1998, 1999, 2000) has described how teachers from the majority culture can become more skilled at incorporating students' home cultures and experiences into classroom instruction. Schmidt (1999) describes how teachers were instructed in using the "ABC's of Cultural

Understanding and Communication," first as a personal experience and then with their own students.

The model requires participants to write an autobiography and then engage in a dialogue or interview with someone from a different culture. When the teachers engaged in the model as a personal experience, they were required to interview or dialogue with a parent to gather information about the parent's life story and views on education, and to gain insights into the student's home. The teachers also shared their own life experiences. An atmosphere of partnership was created. Information sharing was often useful for generating instructional interventions.

Schmidt (2000) describes a scenario with a student from India. Interviewing the parent helped the teacher identify gaps in the student's understanding. It became clearer to the teacher why the student did not do his homework. The teacher had noticed that the student often drew ornate designs related to Indian art. Parent and teacher agreed to have the student use drawing to develop reading comprehension and writing through drawing. It was agreed that the parent would ask his son about the drawings. From this conversation, the student was able to generate drafts and then refine his work with assistance from the teacher.

Schmidt (1998 and 1999) also describes how teachers used the ABC Model with their young pupils. The teacher designed literacy lessons, which included biography, autobiography, and cultural analysis. In one particular classroom, the children used Venn diagrams to assist in seeing similarities and differences between themselves and their friends. In this way, unity was created while honoring individual uniqueness. The children also drew portraits of each other accompanied by paragraphs and/or oral presentations. Some of the teachers who used this model also had students compare their reactions to story characters from multicultural literature. Overall, Schmidt and the teachers found the model highly beneficial for developing home/school connections and enhanced opportunities for literacy across the curriculum.

Incorporating culture through the arts

Culturally competent educators use the arts to incorporate the culture of the home and community. The arts are the means by which a people express themselves through music, song, drama, dance, and visual art. Through studying multicultural artists and their work, students can be encouraged to make connections between their own culture and personal experiences. Teachers can examine the ethnic make-up of their students and then consciously include particular artists.

In a country as culturally diverse as the United States, learning about artistic contributions from various groups benefits all students. Floyd

(1999) elaborates on specific ways of developing multicultural understanding through visual art.

- Develop a bulletin board highlighting two artists from the same time period, but from different cultural backgrounds (Floyd, 1999);
- Have students recognize their own family traditions within the works of art (Floyd, 1999); e.g., African-American artist Jacob Lawrence often depicts community scenes in his work; and
- Invite artists from particular traditions into the classroom.

When McCaleb (1994) initiated dialogue with parents (see 4b above), she asked parents about oral traditions including songs. Songs provide a means of making the home language part of the classroom and school environments. While incorporating the home culture, songs and music can promote language skills and literacy (Woodall and Ziembroski, 2004). Songs are often born out of a people's experience or historical eras and events, and therefore can provide a musical connection between culture, tradition, and the history of a people. Some suggestions for including music in the curriculum include the following:

- Have parents and/or students share songs they learned at home and create a classroom song book;
- Research the origins of music such as jazz, which is African-American in origin and uniquely American;
- Compare musical traditions, such as Christmas caroling in the United States. and las posadas in Mexico;
- Compare kinds of songs such as work songs and lullabies across cultures; and
- Use the Internet as a musical resource. For a wide variety of songs and music across the curriculum, access *www.songsforteaching.com*, which includes Multicultural Music and Songs That Build an Appreciation for Diversity.

Other artistic traditions are useful and valuable in incorporating culture into curriculum. By seeking out "hidden resources" (see section 4a above), teachers uncovered areas of expertise within the community. Parents, grandparents, and community members can be resources for artistic traditions that support learning across the curriculum. Examples of some possible "hidden resources" in the community include the following:

- Quilt making (African-American, Hawaiian, and rural American);
- Egg decorating (Ukrainian);
- Mask-making—"vejigantes" (Puerto Rican);
- Dance (Greek, Puerto Rican, Dominican) and movement such as Tai Chi (Chinese); and

- Cut-paper art—"papel picado" (Mexican). *Making Magic Windows* by Carmen Lomas Garza provides instructions on this tradition.

Songs, poems, rhymes, and folktales offer content for dramatic presentations. Combining these genres with dramatization is consistent with the core curriculum. An excellent resource for teachers on the "how-to" of using drama is the book, *Drama of Color: Improvisation with Multiethnic Folklore* (Saldana, 1995). Saldana (1995) explains his purpose and goals in writing the book:

> ...this book is intended as a teacher resource for enhancing children's ethnic literacy through drama. Folklore from different ethnic groups can be used as a springboard for examining different ethnic perspectives and world goals...My personal goal for drama with children is not to develop formal acting skills but...to provide each participant with personal insight into the multiethnic world in which we live. (Saldana, 1995, p. xii)

Selecting and using materials

Culturally competent educators select materials that are connected to the students' home cultures. The materials that teachers select convey implicit messages to students about what is valued. When teachers choose to present literature, arts, and the scientific or historical contributions from different cultures, they are letting students know that they respect and appreciate the "gifts" different cultures have given to us all. Selecting materials with intention and developing instructional activities based on these materials enables teachers to incorporate students' cultures. Two examples of such materials are as follows.

- *Family Pictures* by Carmen Lomas Garza is a book written by a nationally recognized Mexican-American artist. The illustrations and bilingual text demonstrate daily life experiences within a Mexican-American family and community. This could serve as a springboard for students to do their own writing and illustrating.
- *A Chorus of Cultures* by Alma Flor Ada and colleagues is a program of encouraging literacy through multi-cultural poetry. The program for 365 days includes poems, and some songs and music, drawn from many cultural traditions and is accompanied by suggestions for instructional activities.

CONCLUSION

Several strategies have been presented to enable teachers to incorporate the social and cultural contributions of family into curriculum and instruction. If we are to improve the education process of CLD students and their families, we must be willing to learn more about them and from them.

Culturally competent teachers recognize and see their students and their families as resources for teaching and learning. Lydia Cortes, a former educator turned writer who entered the U.S. public schools in the 1940's after arriving from Puerto Rico, writes of a teacher who made a positive difference:

> Miss Powell made it possible for me to expand my knowledge of English, but more important through my experience with her, she made it possible for me to expand my perceptions and attitudes about teachers, about what learning really can be. I came to understand that you can learn another language and about another culture without being expected to ridicule or reject the one you came into at birth. I learned that some teachers could be interested enough in me to learn about me and from me and to appreciate my world, my language, my culture. And that made it safe for me to appreciate the other world, theirs. (Cortes, 2003, pp. 16–17)

REFERENCES

Ada, A.F., Harris, V., and Hopkins, L. (1993). *A chorus of cultures: Developing multicultural literacy through poetry.* Carmel, CA: Hampton-Brown Books.

Atunez, B. (2004). *Reading and English language learners.* U.S. Dept. of Education, Office of Special Education, *www.readingrockets.org.*

Bode, P. (2003). Puerto Rican art in a social context. In S. Nieto (Ed.), *What keeps good teachers going?* (pp. 82–85). New York: Teachers College Press.

Castellano, J. (1997). Assessing Limited English Proficient students as candidates for special education services, in *NABE News,* Sept. 15, 1997, pp.13–16.

Cortes, L. (2003). In praise of good teachers with love. In G.W. Gayles (Ed.), *In praise of our teachers with love: A multicultural tribute to those who inspired us* (pp.11–21). Boston: Beacon Press.

Floyd, M. (1999). Multicultural understanding through culturally and personally relevant art curricula (part one and part two), in the *National Art Education Association Advisory,* Spring 1999.

Freeman, Y., Freeman, D., and Mercuri, S. (2003). Supporting older bilingual students. *NY SABE Journal, 14,* Spring 2003, pp. 1–18.

Garza, C. L., (1990). *Family Pictures/Cuadros de Familia.* San Francisco, CA: Children's Book Press.

Garza, C. L. (1999). *Making Magic Windows.* San Francisco, CA: Children's Book Press.

Kohl, H. (1995). *I won't learn from you: And other thoughts on creative maladjustment.* New York, NY: New Press.

LAB at Brown University. (2002). Culture, teaching and learning in *The Diversity Kit.* Providence, RI.

McCaleb, S.P. (1994). *Building communities of learners: A collaboration among teachers, students, families, and community.* New York, NY; St. Martin's Press.

Montgomery, W. (2001). Creating culturally responsive, inclusive classrooms. *Teaching Exceptional Children*, March/April 2001, pp. 4–9.

Moran, C. and Tinajero, J. et.al. (1993). Strategies for Working with Overage Students. In A.F. Ada (Ed.), *The Power of Two Languages*. New York, NY: MacMillan/McGraw Hill.

National Association for the Education of Young Children (NAEYC). (1998, July). Learning to read and write: Developmentally appropriate practices for young children, a joint position statement of the International Reading Association. *Young Children*, pp. 30–46.

National Association for the Education of Young Children (1996, January). NAEYC position statement: Responding to linguistic and cultural diversity—recommendations for effective early childhood education. *Young Children*, pp. 4–12.

New York State Education Department. *English Language Arts Resource Guide With Core Curriculum*, p. 21. *www.nysed.gov.*

New York State Education Department. "Grade 3: Communities Around The World—Learning About People and places." *Social Studies Resource Guide with Core Curriculum*, p. 25. *www.nysed.gov.*

North Central Regional Educational Laboratory. (1994). *Funds of knowledge: A look at Moll's research into hidden family resources. www.ncrel.org/sdrs/cityschl.*

Piaget, J. (1973). *To understand is to invent: The future of education.* New York, NY: Grossman. (Originally the work was published in 1948 by UNESCO and was entitled *The Right To Education In the Real World.*)

Rohmer, H. (Ed.) (1997). *Just like me: Stories and portraits by fourteen artists.* San Francisco, CA: Children's Book Press.

Rohmer, H. (Ed.) (1999). *Honoring our ancestors: Stories and pictures by fourteen artists.* San Francisco, CA: Children's Book Press

Saldana, J. (1995). *Drama of color: Improvisation with multiethnic folklore.* Portsmouth, NH: Heineman.

Schmidt, P. (1998). The ABC model: Teachers connect home and school. *National Reading Conference Yearbook*, pp. 194–208.

Schmidt, P. (1999). Focus on research: know thyself and understand others. *Language Arts, 76*(4), March issue, pp. 332–340.

Schmidt, P. (2000). Teachers connecting and communicating with families for literacy development. *National Reading Conference Yearbook*, pp. 195–208.

Thomas, W. and Collier, V. (1997). *School effectiveness for language minority students.* National Clearinghouse for Bilingual Education. Washington, DC: George Washington University, Center for the Study of Language Education.

USA TODAY. Cover Story. (July 2, 2003). "The Face of the American Teacher," p. 1D.

Woodall, L. and Ziembruski, B. (2004). "Promoting Literacy Through Music" in S. Ruth Harris *Songs For Teaching. www.songsforteaching.com/lb/literacymusic.htm.*

TEACHER ACTIVITIES

How can teachers incorporate the cultural and social contributions of family into curriculum and instruction?

Providing Culturally Responsive Instruction

Select a folktale that reflects the ethnic and cultural make-up of your class. Using the sample for strategy #1 as a model, create a lesson plan (or plans) and learning activities based on the folktale. Make sure your instructional activities include ways in which the tale demonstrates the values of the culture. Describe how the lesson and activities align with the district and/or state curriculum. As an additional resource you may use *Drama of color: improvisation with multiethnic folklore* by J. Saldana (1995), cited in the reference list.

Autobiography and biography from students and parents provide a means of connecting life at home and at school. As a variation of this approach, create a student/parent class theme book or individual books based on a universal topic (e.g. my favorite toy/game, first day of school, etc.). Explain why you have chosen this theme. Tell how you will collect the information from your students' families (e.g. develop interview form with students to be administered as a homework assignment, interview parents directly, etc.). Describe how you will publish this information. How will you include families and students with limited English proficiency in this project? Include a statement about how this project meets the goals and objectives of the curriculum.

Teachers as Cultural Researchers

Design a research interview. Conduct the interview with someone at your school who is from your students' home culture. What kinds of questions will you ask that will help you learn about the culture? What kinds of questions will you ask that will assist in instructional planning?

Make a home visit. Choose a parent with whom you have established communication and rapport. Explain that as part of your professional development (or as part of a course) you want to learn more about families and cultures. Ask if you can make a home visit or ask if they can recommend a community center or event you can attend. Prepare a written observation of your visit. Be sure to include what you learned, anything that surprised you, and how this information will impact what you do in the classroom.

Supporting the Home Language

Make a list of ways you can design your classroom environment so that it shows respect for the home language.

Make a list of ways you can show you are supportive of the home language. Choose one way, implement this approach and write a description of the outcome (e.g. have a student, parent, or colleague teach something in or about the home language).

Instructional Activities and Curriculum Which Incorporate Students' Culture

Select one of the approaches described in this section (Tapping Hidden Family and Community Resources, Parents As Partners and Authors, Using Biography and Autobiography to Make Connections). Read additional information on the approach you have selected (see references). Write a general description of the approach. Prepare a plan for using the approach in your classroom.

Invite a parent, community member, or colleague to teach or co-teach an art form or artistic tradition from a particular culture. (You may also invite families to participate in this art activity). What kind of planning might be necessary in advance so that this activity is successful? Host an art show, performance or demonstration to show what students have learned. Have students and families tell or write about the experience.

Selecting and Using Materials

Family Pictures by Carmen Lomas Garza paints family life in the Mexican-American community using words and illustrations (see references). Using the book as a model, create a book or a visual presentation (e.g. power point presentation) about family activities with your class. You can include illustrations and descriptions from both students and their families.

Honoring Our Ancestors: Stories and Pictures by Fourteen Artists, by Harriet Rohmer (editor) is a collection of essays and illustrations, by artists from various cultures (see references). Each artist expresses gratitude to an ancestor who made a positive contribution to the artist's life. Some ancestors are family members (parent, grandparent, etc.) others are "spiritual ancestors" such as predecessors, teachers, etc. Engage your students in a discussion of the word ancestor. Read some selections from the book. Use the book as a model for students to create their own ways of honoring their ancestors, through writing/illustration (as in the book), storytelling about the ancestor, dramatic presentations, etc.

CHAPTER 4

ACTIVITIES TO EMPOWER PARENTS AS COLLABORATORS IN THEIR CHILDREN'S EDUCATION

Amanda Fenlon
Assistant Professor—SUNY Oswego

"Education is too important to be left solely to the educators."

—Francis Keppel

"I am just sick about this! It's eating me up inside!" one mother explained in an emotional phone call to a school administrator in January, the year before her son was to enter school. Jason was an energetic, beautiful, four-year-old child who possessed a winning smile and could demonstrate solid school readiness skills daily to his pre-school teachers. He knew alphabet letters/

Preparing Educators to Communicate and Connect with Families and Communities, pages 47–57
Copyright © 2005 by Information Age Publishing
All rights of reproduction in any form reserved.

sounds, colors, and numerals 1–10. He also had significant language, sensory processing, and behavioral challenges for which he would require special education services and supports in kindergarten. His mother was very anxious about his transition from an inclusive pre-school setting to "real school," and she articulately expressed her angst: "I don't think his pre-school is preparing him for the demands of kindergarten! And they don't listen to me! I'm so afraid he won't be accepted in school! What can I do?"

This scenario actually occurred, but pseudonyms have been used to protect the confidentiality of the family. It clearly illustrates the anxiety, distrust, and lack of knowledge that families may have about schools and school district staff. It points out how a lack of communication can create anxiety and misunderstandings. It raises many questions with regard to preparing teachers to engage with families, such as the following.

- How can we empower parents from the very start to successfully collaborate with teachers and school staff in their child's education program?
- How can we build trust, understanding, and acceptance with families so that they will feel empowered to collaborate with school staff?
- What activities can we engage in to empower families to feel that they are valuable members of a collaborative team that educates their child?
- What ongoing activities can occur that continually engage and empower families to collaborate with school staff on behalf of their children?
- How can we prepare teachers to engage parents in empowering and meaningful activities that will enhance their child's education?

In this section, we will look closely at ways to empower parents. We will point out specific examples of empowering practices that have been used successfully in schools and in teacher preparation programs.

BUILD A RELATIONSHIP RIGHT FROM THE VERY BEGINNING

If we start from the beginning to develop a relationship with families, we can often look at the child's entrance to kindergarten. This is most often a family's first experience with formal schooling. The previous scenario repeats itself, in different variations, every year for families whose children will enter kindergarten.

Research has shown that the entrance of a child into kindergarten can be both a joyful, yet anxious, time for families. Pianta & Kraft-Sayre (1999) noted that a majority of parents (53%) included in a recent study felt positively about their child's transition to school, yet up to 35% of families noted some degree of anxiety about their child's entrance into school. Children's behavioral and emotional difficulties, reluctance to go to school, family adjustment problems, and unrealistic expectations by school personnel were noted as parental concerns. A child's ability to separate from parents, get along with and be liked by peers and teachers, and even to be safe on the school bus can also be causes for parental concern.

What kinds of activities can families and school staff engage in from the very beginning that will empower, and build trust, respect, and collaboration?

- Offer school-based, "town-meeting" style information sessions on kindergarten for families during the spring prior to the start of school. Include such topics as: kindergarten curriculum and expectations; typical daily schedule; transportation information; special services or programs the school offers; and a question-and-answer session. Then allow parents and teachers to break into small groups for more detailed specific questions and concerns. Have parents who have been through the process act as presenters and group facilitators.
- Conduct kindergarten screenings as an exchange of information regarding the child's abilities, strengths, needs, and learning styles. Parents could be asked at registration to be ready to share this information with school staff when the child returns for the screening appointment.
- Let families visit a kindergarten classroom and talk with the teacher in a way that is not disruptive to the teacher or present class.
- Kindergarten teachers can conduct home visits to families or invite families to meet in a neutral location (public library, coffee shop) to discuss their child prior to the start of school. With this face-to-face meeting, teachers can empower parents to share valuable information regarding their child (interests, strengths, needs, learning style). They can forge a bond with the family and let them know how much their participation matters in the overall success of the child's school program.
- Allow families time to come into the school and classroom prior to the actual first day of school. Teachers can extend an invitation for visits during the week in the summer that they are preparing their classrooms.
- Schools can host a kindergarten community-building event before the first day of school. Examples of such events are a barbeque, picnic, or ice cream party in a neighborhood park with "getting-to-know-you" activities for children and families.

Parents of children with significant disabilities most certainly share previously discussed common concerns about entry into kindergarten, but also have concerns specifically relating to how, when, where, and by whom, special services will be provided. In addition, the possibility of losing strong support systems established through pre-school programs may cause parents of children with disabilities to worry (Wolery, 1999). Thus, the entrance into school for these children can be exceedingly more complex and anxiety-laden for their families, and as such, requires a collaborative approach on the parts of all involved (family, receiving and sending teachers and related service staff, and school administrators). It is important to note that in order for families of children with disabilities to feel empowered and part of their school community, they need to be invited to partake in all the activities described previously. In addition, other steps can be taken and activities engaged in to empower parents of young children with disabilities as they transition to school (Fenlon, in press).

- Each November, a friendly letter is sent to all families of children receiving special education services who will be eligible for kindergarten the following year. (See Appendix B.) A welcoming phone call from a school district administrator follows the letter, if a parent does not respond.
- In response to letter and follow-up phone contacts, families become part of the decision making collaborative team. Parents and pre-school staff make observations of kindergarten classrooms and meet kindergarten teachers, related services staff, and the school principal. Informal collaborative meetings take place.
- School district staff observes the child in the pre-school classroom. Both school staff and family gather and share information (various teaching strategies, materials, or assistive technology that the child may require) to prepare for the child's entrance into kindergarten. (February–April)
- Additional collaborative meetings occur with parents, and sending and receiving teams, if necessary, to discuss proposed kindergarten recommendations and services. (April)
- The Annual Review and Initial School Age Special Education meeting occurs. All collaborating team members (parents, sending and receiving teams, district administrator, and parent representative) attend and participate. The Individualized Education Plan (IEP) is developed collaboratively. (April–June)
- The family participates in typical kindergarten orientation activities (screening, opening picnic, or other events). Additional observations of the child occur, if needed, to further develop relationships and gather updated information prior to the child's first day of school. (July–August)

It seems crucial to note the necessity of administrative support, both at the building and district level, for these activities that promote empowerment of parents. Without the leadership of principals and district administrators, activities to engage families will not happen.

Families of pre-schoolers with disabilities who participated in this collaborative transition process felt empowered as expressed in their own words.

"Parents talking to teachers is so important, and they need to hear from us. As a parent, I know my child best, and what they need. Getting to share that with his future teachers and therapists was absolutely necessary."

"Seeing the classroom was fantastic! It put me at ease. I couldn't have made an intelligent decision without going to observe and talking together with everyone."

"There's no question that I felt a big part of the process."

"I felt comforted by us all working together on my child's behalf."

The parent in the opening scenario is now engaged in the collaborative steps for her son's successful transition to school and although still anxious, she undoubtedly feels more empowered than when she placed the original phone call.

"KNOWLEDGE IS POWER"—FAMILIES TEACHING AND LEARNING FOR EMPOWERMENT

"Knowledge is power." We all know this old but important adage. When individuals and groups share knowledge with one another, they are essentially sharing power. Therefore, the more knowledge parents can gain and the more they can share with teachers, the more they are empowered. Several examples of empowering parents through teaching and learning are described below.

Families as Learners

- One important way to empower parents within schools is to include them in staff development activities both as learners and as teachers. Many school districts in New York State invite families to participate free of charge in school district professional development workshops. Mailings with conference registration forms, topics, and descriptions are sent to all families in the school district, and they are encouraged to attend.

- Teachers and schools empower parents by providing them with up-to-date information on best educational practices they are using, such as new literacy or math programs, and diversity and inclusion programs that will benefit all children. Teachers, especially special educators, need to be able to provide parents with easily understood information on the special education system and families' rights within that system, especially the specifics of the Individuals with Disabilities Education Act (IDEA). Provisions should be made for non-literate parents and guardians to receive this information as well. Other means of sharing information might include meetings, phone calls, or jointly viewing and discussing informational videotapes. Special educators also need to be able to connect families with needed community resources, such as respite, advocacy, and support groups.

- For the child's learning to be further enhanced, special educators can share new and promising teaching strategies that parents might find helpful at home (i.e., using visual strategies with children with autism). Sharing knowledge with parents shouldn't necessarily mean just sending flyers and handouts home in a child's backpack. It should consist of more meaningful opportunities to learn together, such as cooperative study groups and/or attending conferences together, with financial assistance and childcare available if needed.

Families as Teachers

- Maybe most importantly, parents feel empowered when they teach others. When school districts invite parents to present as part of their staff development efforts, this has the wonderful impact of reaching in-service teachers directly. An example is a mother-and-son team presenting to teachers on learning characteristics and successful teaching strategies for students with Asperger's Syndrome. This mother-son team was able to present valuable information and personal perspectives based upon years of experience with the disorder and with schools.

- Parents of different cultures, including Native American, Hispanic, Asian, and others can take an active role in presenting parental perspectives in professional development opportunities for teachers that focus on family engagement. In California, "mentor parents" provide professional development to school staff on parent involvement in schools, including parents' negative past experiences that discourage participation, and perceived teacher biases based on parents' different socioeconomic status, race, gender, physical appearance, or language ability (U.S. Department of Education, Family Involvement, 1997).

Family as Faculty in Teacher Education Programs

- Teacher preparation programs are using the expertise of parents in training future teachers to engage with families. Families are co-instructors at the University of South Florida in a project entitled "Family as Faculty." The university recruits family members as guest lecturers in education classes with the goal of enhancing "home-school partnerships by providing future educators with opportunities to listen to the voices of families from a variety of walks of life" (Family as Faculty, 2000). According to Dr. Jane Sergay, topics presented by parents have included attention deficit disorder, language barriers, socioeconomic barriers, teacher conferences, and grandparent caregiving. Parents recruited for the program are provided a three-day orientation and training during which they reflect on their experiences, identify specific issues and personal stories, and consider what makes a good presentation. They also give practice presentations and give one another feedback. Parents receive a training stipend and fee for each presentation. This program is now being replicated at other institutions, including the University of North Carolina and the University of Central Florida.
- Special educators striving to teach students with disabilities in general education/inclusive classrooms often need the family's advocacy skills and power to create systemic change in school districts where inclusion has not been a reality. Families that belong to advocacy and respite/support groups, such as Exceptional Family Resources in Syracuse, New York, can teach pre-service special educators important skills in advocating for inclusive placements for their students and the value of connecting families with other parents and community service and support agencies. Many universities such as SUNY Oswego (New York) and Syracuse University routinely partner with such groups to allow the expertise of parents to influence pre-service teachers.

FAMILIES EMPOWERED THROUGH COLLABORATION

Family interviews

For children with significant disabilities, research tells us that teachers must develop a strong and collaborative partnership with families in order to create and implement a meaningful IEP. Indeed, the reauthorization of the Federal law IDEA stresses increased "parent participation" at every stage of the special education process from referral to assessment to program development and review. IDEA guarantees parents access to all records, requires written consent for evaluations and placement, and strongly encourages major involvement in the development and review of the child's IEP. In order to prepare teachers for this expectation, professors at the University of New Mexico's undergraduate Program in Special Education fund families to share specific experiences regarding their children receiving special education services and to allow students to get to know and interview them.

One such interviewing tool that helps families and special educators plan and develop a vision for the child's future in inclusive classrooms and typical community settings is Choosing Options and Accommodations for Children (COACH), created by Giangreco, Cloninger, and Iverson. COACH begins with a structured interview with the family to discover their priorities for their son or daughter in areas such as: (1) being safe and healthy; (2) having a home, now and in the future; (3) having choice and control to match one's age and culture; (4) having meaningful relationships; and (5) participating in meaningful activities in various places. Then the family provides information on various skills (communication, socialization, personal management, leisure/recreation, selected academics, home, school, community, and vocational) needed for participation in current and future settings.

The COACH interview can be structured, yet open-ended and family-directed, and is an excellent way for teachers to truly discover what parents' priorities really are, and then to incorporate these priorities into the child's IEP. Many teacher preparation programs such as SUNY Oswego (New York) and St. Michael's College (Vermont) incorporate COACH into course assignments and field practicum. Pre-service teachers who have had the experience of interviewing families using the COACH process have said that "it was worth the cost of tuition!" and "one of the most valuable things I have done as a graduate student" to be able to learn the parents' powerful perspectives and gain valuable information that will enhance my teaching. Most importantly, students have remarked that conducting a family interview which allows families to articulate goals and priorities for their children will be something that they will "definitely do" when they become practicing teachers

Meet Families Where They're at ... and Carefully Listen to Them

Finally, one of the most simple, yet powerful, tools that we need to train teachers to use in empowering families is the ability to listen to them (Davern, 1996; Hornby, 2000; Muscott, 2002; O'Shea, O'Shea, Algozzine & Hammitte, 2001). The practice of active listening, being able to convey educational information with genuine sincerity in a sensitive and empathic manner, and to continually convey the value of the child to parents is not easily taught to pre-service teachers. Role-playing and follow-up critiques of parent conferences and IEP planning meetings can be helpful tools to teach these skills and values.

If families are from a culture or race different from their own, teachers need to be able to honestly and openly communicate with them to understand, respect, and value their cultural differences. This typically requires teachers to have a good grounding of their own culture and biases. Ruggiano Schmidt (1998) advocates for improved communication between teachers and parents through a process known as the ABC's of cultural understanding and communication. Using this process, teachers complete an autobiography (A), biography (B), and cross-cultural analysis (C) to help them develop improved cultural understanding and communication with students' families.

CONCLUSION

In this section, we have presented ways to empower families to interact with the school as collaborators in their children's education. We have talked about empowering families from the very beginning by encouraging collaboration and shared decision making as their children enter school. We have presented ideas for empowerment through the attainment and sharing of knowledge by families, both learning and teaching within schools and within teacher preparation programs. We have discussed the importance of talking constructively and openly with families about what priorities they have for their children's futures and being able to include them in the development of educational plans. Finally, we have stressed the simple, yet sometimes elusive, skill of being able to truly listen to families, and to genuinely convey to them the value of their children.

REFERENCES

Davern, L. (1996, April). Listening to parents of children with disabilities. *Educational Leadership, 53*(7), 61–63.

Family as faculty. (2000, Fall). *FINE Forum e-Newsletter.* Retrieved September 2, 2002, from: *www.gse.harvard.edu.hfrp/projects/fine/fineforum/index.html.*

Fenlon, A. (in press). Paving the way to kindergarten for young children with disabilities: Collaborative steps for a successful transition to school. *Young Children.*

Giangreco, M., Cloninger, C., & Iverson, G. (2000). *Choosing options and accommodations for children: A guide to planning for students with disabilities (COACH-2).* Baltimore: Paul H. Brookes.

Hornby, G. (2000). *Improving parental involvement.* New York: Cassell.

Individuals with Disabilities Education Act Amendments of 1997, 20 U.S.C.S. 140.

Muscott, H.S. (2002, Winter). Exceptional partnerships: Listening to the voices of families. *Preventing School Failure,* 4692, 66–69.

O'Shea, D.J., O'Shea, L.J., Algozzine, R., & Hammitte, D.J. (2001). *Families and teachers of individuals with disabilities: Collaborative orientations and responsive practices.* Boston: Allyn & Bacon.

Pianta, R.C. & Kraft-Sayre, M. (1999). Parents' observations about their children's transitions to kindergarten. *Young Children, 54*(3), pp. 47–52.

Schmidt, P. (1998). The ABC model: Teachers connect home and school. *National Reading Conference Yearbook,* 194–208.

U.S. Department of Education. (1997). *Family involvement in children's education: Successful local approaches.* Washington, DC: Office of Educational Research and Improvement.

Wolery, M. & Wilbers, J.S. (Eds.), (1994). *Including children with special needs in early childhood programs,* Vol. 6. Washington, DC: National Association for the Education of Young Children.

TEACHER ACTIVITIES

Extend Your Learning

1. Attend an advocacy group meeting of parents of children with disabilities. Talk with the parents about their perspectives regarding their children's most effective and caring teachers. What can you learn from these parents that will make you the best teacher you can be?

2. Identify a local public school that is known for exemplary parent-teacher relationships and attend one of their PTA meetings. What do you observe about the interaction between parents and teachers? What do you observe about the balance of power and sharing of ideas between parents and teachers? What kinds of activities are planned/discussed and what does this tell you about the partnerships that exist at this school?

3. If you are a current special education teacher, offer to make a home visit to the parent(s) of your students to learn more about what priorities they have for their child for the upcoming year. Ask them what they see as their child's strengths, learning style and educational needs. Ask them to tell you anything they wish about their child to assist you in teaching them effectively.

CHAPTER 5

POSITIVE LEADERSHIP FOR FAMILY ENGAGEMENT

Peter L. Kozik
School Administrator and Doctoral Student
Syracuse University

"The child is not only a voter and a subject of law; he is also...a member of a family, himself responsible...in turn, for rearing and training of future children..."

—John Dewey

"Candor is a compliment; it implies equality. It's how true friends talk."

—Peggy Noonan

I had assumed a principalship in an area of the State marked by high poverty, seasonal jobs, and a keen suspicion of outsiders. The building where I worked experienced a 49% free and reduced lunch rate. As frequently happens in a principal's life, I was working late in a second-floor office, making

Preparing Educators to Communicate and Connect with Families and Communities, pages 59–75

telephone calls and finishing paperwork from the day's events. I was walking around my desk to retrieve a file from a table on which I spread out my work, when the door to my office banged open from a forceful kick, about waist high. The mother of a student I had just suspended stormed into my office, fiercely railing against me. Behind her strode her sister from out-of-town, equally fierce and agitated. They each pointed their fingers and screamed choice expletives and epithets at me in rapid succession. It was at that point that I made one of the smartest moves of my career: I sat down.

The vignette is an extreme, albeit true, example of the situations that principals and other school leaders face. It serves to exemplify the frequently precarious, often times heated, and occasionally dangerous, relationships that school leaders have with families. Every seasoned administrator can testify to being lambasted by a student's caregiver over the phone or in person. Principals and school superintendents frequently hear what can't, and won't, be said to the student's teachers. Administrators serve as lightning rods for parental frustration and discontent. As figures of authority in the district, school administrators stand out as targets for ire.

My initial reaction to this situation illustrates a key first principle in developing positive relationships with families: developing service leadership. Administrators, more than any other school district employee, must practice the notion of serving the public. I chose not to confront the women who had just barged into my office. Instead, I diffused an otherwise explosive state of affairs by lowering myself as a target with the recognition that, from her viewpoint, this mother in my office had a legitimate complaint, however she expressed it. As a servant to this particular taxpayer in the district, I was accountable, first, to listen.

Arguably, the woman's behavior, which was mirrored by her child whom I had suspended, was so inappropriate that to hear her through would seem ludicrous. For some administrators, the threat may have been perceived as too great with which to deal, and the intervention of law enforcement might well have been threatened and then acted upon. The consequence of this choice would most likely have been continued escalation, possible reprisal, and the loss of credible contact with a family and a troubled young person. Every administrator must weigh the risks of screaming back, shutting the door, or hanging up the phone. Unless a plan of reconnecting with the family is made and the administrator sees the opportunity for service leadership after communication is severed, the prospect of a positive outcome for the child and his caregivers is dim.

Although service leadership is currently being defined, researchers have broken down the component parts to stimulate continued thinking and learning in this field. The component parts that have been expressed are: vision, trust, credibility, service, and influence (Farling, Stone and Winston, 1999). Each has its roots in the thinking and the literature about leadership. Each is essential to engaging families successfully.

VISION

The ability to elucidate and craft an ideal toward which a community can strive is an essential component of good leadership. Providing the school's vision, however, can be difficult, and sharing the vision with constituencies can be daunting. The key to a successful school vision is the "bedrock belief" of the leader (Goldberg, 2001). In order for a school to grow toward an ideal, the ideal must be firmly rooted in the administrator's belief system as well as in the current reality of the situation (Collins, 2001).

Beliefs about family engagement connect deeply to an administrator's personal beliefs about him or herself and about education. Before undertaking a program of family engagement, an administrator should take the time to reflect on personal values and on how willing he or she is to accept families into the school and the district.

- How do you, as an administrator, honestly feel about having parents and families in your school? The ambition to become an administrator is fueled by many sources, not the least of which are the desire for financial remuneration and the desire for prestige, power, and control.
- How comfortable are you working with children and their families? Knowing your students and their families is the foundation to engaging with them successfully.
- How aware are you of the complexities of cultural and race relations in your community? An administrator's own background impacts on relations with families.
- What do you believe about race, poverty, and culture? An administrator's own experience of school and the dominant culture impacts on relations with families.
- Are you aware of a deficit view in your outlook on any individual, class, race, gender, sexual preference, or disability? A viable and adaptable self-assessment instrument is available in Winifred Montgomery's *Creating Culturally Responsive, Inclusive Classrooms* (2001).

Particularly as educational leaders, we must be rid of the all-or-nothing approach to education. A helpful question to ask is: What part of the challenge of successfully engaging families do I own?

The reality of the situation means that an administrator must take stock of the families he or she is dealing with. An informal poll of parents as they undertake business with the school might yield important understandings.

Ask: "When is the best time of day to have parent-teacher conferences?" Or better: "How can our school better connect with your family?" A formal survey might contribute further to enhancing the school's understanding of families and of efforts at engagement. The survey can be provided at concerts, sporting events, PTA meetings, banquets, and budget votes. Invite families to answer questions together on the district's website. Questions might include: "Describe the ideal level of connection between your home and school. How does the school communicate effectively with your home? What are some of the ways that the school can better communicate? How would you rate the quality of education this school provides your child? What changes would you like to see to better serve you and your child?"

- Make efforts to connect with families public.
- Announce them at school functions, publish the survey in the district newsletter, and encourage the press to consider covering your efforts.
- Enlist the help of interested and active parents to telephone constituents for deeper and better understanding.
- Involve board of education members directly in communicating with parents in the district. The vision for successful family engagement begins with complete openness and transparency in school governance, and boards can benefit from district-initiated contact with constituents.

The Onondaga Central School District (OCSD), under the leadership of Dr. Timothy Barstow, has instituted a committee composed of parents and community members to discuss and to recommend action regarding the school budget. Voluntary membership on the committee is extended through the school district newsletter and includes board of education members. The committee meets over the course of several months to analyze expenses, to understand revenue sources, to consider the upcoming tax levy, and to advise the board of education about the results of its work. The committee assures that the interests of taxpayers in the district are balanced against the need for a quality education for its children. The committee structure creates a core of budget advocates in the community that can speak to the proposed budget expertly, concretely, and directly. Families are engaged, therefore, at a meaningful level in the operation of the district. Subsequent superintendents in OCSD have continued to use the committee model.

Finally, all personnel in a district including teaching assistants, bus drivers, cafeteria workers, custodians, and support staff should be given professional development opportunities to increase awareness and effectiveness in working with cultural diversity and successfully engaging families (The Diversity Kit). There is also benefit to coming to know each student in your school as well and as completely as possible, which means knowing their families. Family engagement encourages student achievement. Feuerstein (2000) reports several studies that document the academic benefits of parental involvement in schools. The bedrock belief of successfully engaging families in their children's education is that involving families is good for children.

TRUST

Although the scenario at the beginning of this section seems extreme, it illustrates an important lesson about trust. The continued relationship with the mother in the narrative depends foremost on valuing her as an individual. Trust begins with valuing people and valuing people's ideas and experiences. As an administrator, it is important to extend trust, from which trust flows back in return (Martin, 1998). Trust develops through acceptance and respect and their communication to constituents. Acceptance and respect develop through careful listening. Trust continues in a positive climate of personal encouragement and collaborative problem solving.

Trust becomes instilled first in a school by observing confidentiality for all students. Although students with special needs should always be protected by adherence to the regulations governing confidentiality, the same holds true for all students and their families. Conversations about children at the front desk, with secretarial staff, between teachers in the hallway, with parents in the front foyer, even in faculty rooms, should be brought behind closed doors into secure private areas. Like health care workers, school personnel must observe strict limits on any public conversations regarding children, their academic progress or its lack, their families, or their personal situations.

The issue of trust is particularly crucial when working with the parents and families of minority students (Harry, 1992). Years of disempowerment of parents of minority youngsters and the struggle for fair and equal opportunity linger in the background of almost every conversation with minority families. Distrust of the dominant culture makes the need for respecting and inviting parents of minority youngsters into conversations about their children and about school all the more important. Likewise, studies have documented the disparity between the views and perceptions of educators on parents of lower socioeconomic strata and on those in more affluent families (Shepard & Rose, 1995). Given time and empathy, all parents are able to provide keen insight into their children and to help develop policies, practices, and school experiences that are relevant and ultimately beneficial. The first step is to trust parents of color, all parents, when it comes to their thinking about their children in your care. Once trust is given and received, the path and pattern of trusting can be established.

> The principal at LaFayette Jr./Sr. High School, worked deliberately to build trust by ensuring that all children's voices were heard and all cultures were honored. The LaFayette School District encompasses the Onondaga Nation Territory south of Syracuse, NY, and the population at the high school includes 27% native people. Beginning in 1999, the school instituted events such as Native American social dances, with performers from the Iroquois Confederacy, in which the entire school participates. The success of these events has led to cultural fairs and week-long cultural celebrations during which speakers from various traditions, ethnicities, and cultural viewpoints raise student awareness. The foods of Korean, Arabic, Native, Irish, and other cultures are shared along with cultural creations and accomplishments. Over the next two years, native people were routinely included in discussions about the various communities at Lafayette, including the impact of substance abuse and bias against minorities.
>
> As a result of these early efforts at developing cultural responsiveness, in 2003, the LaFayette District experienced an historic moment: the raising of the Haudenoshonee flag at the Jr./Sr. High School along side the American flag (Figure 5.1). Superintendent Mark Mondinaro, supported by a board of education on which served the first-ever elected Native American member, emphasized the fairness and correctness of such a gesture in honor of the students and families from a recognized sovereign nation.

There is great value in "walking the talk" when it comes to schools that are culturally responsive and engage families meaningfully.

Figure 5.1.   The Haudenoshonee flag along side the American flag.

School administrators must help analyze the barriers that are keeping professionals from pursuing collaboration with parents and from connecting to the community. Responsive educators should recognize that all children are culturally bound to their homes, and that this fact can enhance learning for all (NAEYC, 1995). Recognizing that parents, like others, can be blameful and shirk responsibility, educators can focus on concrete examples of behavior at home and school. Discuss actual student work in conferences and at CSE meetings. Look for similarities between parents' experiences and yours, either growing up or as a parent yourself. These attitudes and strategies can help elevate trust. Recognize the strength and support inherent in the social networks developed among parents, particularly those of the same ethnic group. Research how eye contact differs among cultures to avoid misunderstandings (Conderman & Flet, 2001). Provide communication in many forms and in the languages represented in your district, and listen carefully when parents speak.

One of the most critical times when family and school concerns conjoin is at a parent-teacher conference. School leaders need to help educate teachers about best practice in implementing these conferences by, among other things, facilitating fruitful parent-teacher conferences.

- Ensure the comfort of staff and participants. Create adequate time to discuss each child; develop a comfortable environment within which to speak; maintain professionalism and confidentiality; and provide flexible schedules for professional staff to complete this assignment.
- Help teachers organize the meetings. Recognize that teachers frequently work in professional isolation; encourage them to reflect on their practice. Suggest they share ideas about successful and meaningful conference experiences that they have created.
- Knowing the students, and which conferences may prove problematic, offer to sit in on any conference or on particularly difficult ones. Always first ask the staff member, then the family, if you may sit in.
- Make sure, as much as possible, that the number of participants at a conference is known ahead of time to avoid overwhelming one parent or a single family with teamed professionals. Allow families to anticipate numbers.
- Provide the agenda to parents ahead of time. Allow at least twenty minutes, focusing half the conference on the teacher's perspective and half the conference on the parents'.
- Consider initiating student-led conferences (Lawrence-Lightfoot, 2003).
- Provide refreshments and organized child-care. When necessary, provide transportation and alternate meeting sites.

Set the stage for success by being positive about the experience your teachers will provide to parents. These steps pay substantial dividends in reaching the community and bolstering morale among staff.

Unfortunately, the leadership culture in America has created a glorified figure of the individual leader who can go it alone to develop change and to improve organizational performance. Recognize that this romanticized view of leadership begs the issue of a group or organization having within it the seeds of successful change, and a leader's being able to capitalize on fitting "individual talents to the task to be accomplished" (Goldberg, 2001). Likewise, the romanticized leadership culture in America does not easily tolerate mistakes by its leaders. Yet, in a school system, mistakes are an intrinsic part of the learning process. To gain trust, it is important to be able to apologize, to remain flexible, to seek input from others, to renew efforts, and to seek other and myriad possible solutions to problems (Goertz, 2000).

CREDIBILITY

Effective family engagement by committed educational leaders relies heavily on the believability of the professionals involved. Seeing the work of the school first-hand builds credibility and affects believability in the institution. Developing opportunities such as school visitations and classroom shadowing experiences cultivates dialogue with families and community members. The National Education Association has a format available for successfully creating "Back to School" Days.

Credibility is enhanced by school personnel's making the effort to participate in the community outside the school day and by understanding the needs of individual families. Clearly, attendance at sports' events, concerts, award ceremonies, and open houses are critical for administrators as well as for teachers. Become versed in the issues facing the various family configurations outside of school, including foster families, gay and lesbian and blended families, two-career, and single parent families (Diffily, 2004). Guard against negative misconceptions because they weaken credibility; test your assumptions rigorously and regularly. Recognize the fact that every school and every community is culturally diverse regardless of racial or ethnic mix or economic position.

The model of special education services developed by most districts is instructive in building family engagement. What would our schools be like if every child were included in the educational process with an IEP that carried them through from kindergarten to high school graduation? How believable are we as instructional leaders in championing a child's education without involving the child's family? It might be argued that although the more intimate, and hence often fruitful, connections experienced in the CSE are unrealistic for every child in the American system, the recognition of different methods of family engagement is necessary nonetheless. The partnership between school and family and the level of interaction represented by the CSE process is instructive to consider (Davern, 1996). An important question to ask is: In addition to the disabilities that your students have, how much do you as an administrator know about the culturally and class-based diverse styles of childrearing represented in your school population?

Time to work with families is always hard to come by, yet dedication to family engagement as a top priority means that time can be found, and remuneration for time spent is possible. At a middle and secondary level, create teams of teachers whose task it is to oversee the progress of 20 to 30 students in the course of a year and to regularly contact households with positive news, as well as the need for improvement. The effort that a district or school makes in this regard strengthens relations with the community and bolsters credibility. To be credible, a commitment to family engagement needs to be made.

DeRuyter Elementary School has provided weekly congruence time among special and regular education teachers, therapists, the school psychologist, teaching assistants, parents, and the principal to get feedback from home, to evaluate programs, and to guide student progress. For the cost of two substitute teachers, the twenty-minute meetings that take place over two mid-week afternoons, are structured in their agenda and focused on tangible outcomes. Teachers bring samples of student work for quick reference. Parents bring anecdotes from home and journal entries that serve as additional forms of communication. The entire group monitors and adjusts the students' programs regularly, while making special education committee meetings run smoothly and productively.

Credibility is increased when community members and parents witness that efforts are made on their behalf. For example, polling parents for convenient parent-teacher conference times helps bolster a school's family-friendly position. Be aware that among mothers in poverty, 67% cannot leave their job site (Bracey, 2001). Many of them have no means of transportation to get to the school. Recognize that a variety of possible times for conferences *de facto* imply flexible scheduling for professionals and remuneration for time spent beyond the working day.

Support parents in their task of raising children. Discover what parents need to help and support their childrearing efforts. At a faculty meeting or in a teacher observation conference, the moment parents are blamed for their child's not learning or for the school's poor performance, the onus for education can shift away from the professionals whose job it is to teach.

The professional's first response to concern about a child's not learning might be: Was the material taught well? If it was, what evidence is there to know it was taught well? Concerns about a child's behavior might translate into asking: What do you know about this child as an individual and about his learning? How is the classroom organized in terms of time, space, materials, population, and attitude to optimize differentiated instruction and each child's potential? Moreover and more telling, perhaps, the issue for administrators should be: What improvements need to be made in the system to ensure that every child learns well and that teachers feel comfortable taking responsibility for their work?

SERVICE

Serving the children of a school or district and encouraging service by students and community members are key priorities in engaging families. Service means both parents and community members working with the school to enhance learning for children, and it means recognizing that as an administrator, you provide service to children and to the people who pay your salary. This point does not allow for personal abuse, but does however insist on always maintaining professional comportment, and treating every person with respect and value, even though their treatment of you is not immediately respectful.

- Do not discount parents because they do not show up at meetings or at conferences. Take the time to follow-up, and to help teachers follow-up, in ascertaining the issues that create boundaries to parental involvement.
- Ask questions; learn continually.
- Focus on family strengths. Parents enjoy contributing positively.
- Recognize and celebrate parental service, PTA/PTO involvement, support as a room parent, and assistance with school programs. Use the strengths within the community to affect school climate positively, to enhance the successful management of children, and to affect home-life for the benefit of the child and the parent.
- Plan visits to homes. Recognize, in addition, that families struggle with similar issues. Parent-to-parent connections enhance and support student skills and the motivation to succeed.

Fabius-Pompey Middle School has developed a job shadow program for its seventh graders that is overseen by a Volunteer Coordinator, a mother of two middle school students, who was eventually hired by the district to connect students to future job opportunities and to more closely involve the community. Every month, alumni from the school district are invited to return to the school and discuss the jobs they hold, their college and training experiences, and to provide advice about the high school program of study that qualified them for their positions. Students complete interest inventories through which they express their future plans and their career goals. Based on these preferences, these seventh-grade students are assigned daylong job-shadowing experiences that follow their interests. They are advised on dress and comportment.

Students have witnessed open heart surgery at a local hospital, ridden with the local sheriff's department for a day, collected soil samples with the State Department of Environmental Protection, and talked Stealth Bombers into the air as would-be air traffic controllers. Their experiences take place well before their transition planning in eighth grade, and students are able to begin winnowing their preferences before harder decisions need to be made. Based on job shadows, many students become energized for the experience of school and motivated to complete their studies. Community members enjoy the program because they get to share expertise and connect with young people as mentors and as valuable resources in the field. Children enjoy the experience of being in the world of work and reflecting on possible future choices.

Parents and family members can serve as resources in any number of ways, and families can share their expertise with one another and with the school community.

Finally, keep the notion firmly in your own mind that you are a servant of the public. Examine honestly your motivation for becoming an administrator. If financial remuneration, power, control, or prestige is the primary reason for your work in the field, question yourself seriously about your commitment to service. Are you fearful? Are standardized test results and school or district-wide performance the best indicators of how you are helping raise the children of the community you serve? Divest yourself of ego and the romantic notion that leaders function in isolation to create magnificent change. Recognize the "public" in public education. Dedicate yourself to the twenty families in your school who are struggling the most.

INFLUENCE

"Influence is the ability to change another's behaviors" (Einstein & Humphreys, 2001). One of the superintendent's and the board of education's tasks in the community is to help shape school-family, child-centered policy and to assure that policy is connected to practice so that the behaviors of the professionals in the district change, if need be.

As is true with any human institution, the success of a school district is predicated on the strength of its relationship building. Administrators, like teachers, need to make themselves visible in the community. Villa references the need to become proactive within a community of people, as well as to invite civic and other leaders into school for a tour, classes, and a lunch. Creating connections through local service organizations is an important way to draw families and the community into the life of the school. Rotary, Optimists, and Kiwanis are all good conduits for connection to business and community leaders. Don't overlook the local VFW Post, local churches, soup kitchens, and local leagues and sponsors of athletics. Chambers of Commerce, beauty salons, barbershops, and homeowners associations are also viable for connections (Villa, 2003). Finally, make sure you are in touch with and on the mailing lists of local advocacy groups such as those created for minority populations and for individuals with disabilities. Attend the meetings of these organizations and invite these professional leaders into faculty and community meetings at school.

It is often traditional for the principal at the elementary level to regularly issue a newsletter to parents, outlining events and activities at the school, providing summaries of monthly events and field trips, contributing helpful hints about parenting, and reviewing the lunch menu for the coming month. The common belief is that, whereas elementary students will "back-pack" these missives home, middle school and high school students are unlikely to get newsletters into their parents' hands. However, regularly issuing newsletters at the secondary level that review developments at the school, provide current sports and extra-curricular information, and spotlight students and student achievement are welcome additions in households and can strengthen support for secondary programs.

> Cato-Meridian High School developed a bi-monthly newsletter that included several items of interest for parents in addition to announcements, schedules, and calendars. The principal included descriptions of school policies, answered questions that had been raised at board of education and site-based management meetings, and provided information from guidance counselors about eighth-grade transition and college searches. In addition, articles about the value of extra-curricular activities and parenting teenagers were included, as were celebrations of student success and the recognition of student awards given through an extensive character education program. When encouraging student study skills, a family checklist of positive study skills behavior was developed and sent home.

Finally, the allocation of resources toward engaging families meaningfully is a significant step in enhancing district relations and in improving student achievement.

- Requiring that some re-credentialing hours for professional development sought by New York and other states be fulfilled by working with diverse populations and family engagement is a possibility for teacher in-service.

- Continually training and implementing school-based management teams of parents and community members keep the community's learning and commitment fresh.
- Encouraging teachers through a system of mini-grants to connect with at least one parent or community member for a curricular or instructional project strengthens connections between home and school (Swap, 1993).
- Inviting parents to be part of professional development opportunities at the school provides understanding and appreciation.

IMPACT OF FAMILY ENGAGEMENT ON THE PREPARATION OF EDUCATIONAL LEADERS

Schools are unlike corporations, and the task of school leaders is very different from the tasks associated with continuing profit and shareholder satisfaction. Inviting parents into a school is not tantamount to inviting paying customers to walk an assembly line or to visit the cubicles of managers. The likening of children, albeit children routinely tested under standardized conditions, to products that a company creates is ludicrous, and yet this is becoming the prevailing logic among some policy makers. In October 2002, there were 49 million children attending public schools in America (www.census.gov). The sheer number of lives at stake is staggering. Although much can be learned from the corporate leadership literature, a model that emphasizes care, compassion, collaboration, and the engagement of families is critical for developing schools that serve all learners well. Administrators who are child and family-centered, who recognize their place in the community in which they work, and who always listen first must be cultivated (Hoyle & Slater, 2001). The emphasis can and should be on one child and one family at a time.

In the last ten years, a vast body of research has developed around issues relating to family engagement. Only seven states require that administrators understand and promote the means to family engagement and parental involvement (Pipho, 1994). Research indicates that family engagement positively affects student achievement when it is comprehensive, long-lasting, and well planned. Strategic planning for lasting family engagement needs to be part of the educational leadership curriculum, as does training to work with diverse student populations. Curricula should also focus on the myriad practical means of engaging families, on the critical overlap in what teachers are learning and what administrators should know, and on perseverance when it comes to the most reluctant family partners.

Schools should be safe, not just physically safe, but emotionally safe. This means:

- School leaders should be prepared with the ability to develop a comprehensive framework for family engagement.
- All children should be free from bullying and sarcasm by their teachers and by their peers. Every child should be cared for. Educational leaders should be prepared with this curricular focus.
- Setting rules and expectations for respect and professionalism in educational organizations is imperative. Confidentiality in schools is the cornerstone of trust and professionalism. Confidentiality regarding students and families, meaning disallowing conversations about any individuals within earshot of people not directly involved, should be taught and emphasized.
- Being sensitive to issues of race, sexual preference, disability, age, class, and gender bias leads to schools that have the integrity to serve and are welcoming environments for all. These issues should be surfaced and discussed by anyone associated with children's education openly and honestly without fear of judgment or reprisal beginning with educational leaders.
- The value of not knowing an answer immediately should be highlighted. The willingness to say that, as a leader, you will follow-up on a question rather than give an evasive answer cannot be underestimated in the public's regard for its school. Humility is the first value of exceptional leadership (Collins, 2001). Transparency is key. Follow-up is important and publicly valued.

CONCLUSION

Family involvement cannot be left solely to teachers. Proactive administrators can do much to initiate and to cultivate family engagement on multiple levels. Using service leadership as a model, administrators should be willing and able to implement vision, trust, credibility, service, and influence. Being firm in the family-centered direction and purpose of a school, honoring confidentiality and establishing respect, remaining truthful and transparent, acknowledging one's place in the community, and affecting positive attitudes create strong community ties. These ties, in turn, affect and encourage growth, learning, and increased student achievement.

The ideas represented here easily form the basis to develop educational leaders who engage successfully with families. Be clear about your own moral vision for children and their treatment. Remaining child and family-centered is the key to lasting positive impact in buildings, through programs, and at districts.

REFERENCES

Bracey, G. (2001). Research—School involvement and the working poor. *Phi Delta Kappan, 82*(10), 795–797.

Collins, J. (2001). *Good to great: Why some companies make the leap and others don't.* New York, NY: Harper Collins.

Conderman, G., & Flett, A. (2001). Enhance the involvement of parents from culturally and linguistically diverse backgrounds. *Intervention in School and Clinic, 37*(1), 53–58.

Davern, L. (1996). Listening to parents of children with disabilities. *Educational Leadership, 53*(7), 61–64.

Diffily, D. (2004). *Teachers and families working together.* Boston, MA: Allyn & Bacon.

Einsten, W.O., & Humphreys, J.H. (2001). Transforming leadership: Matching diagnostics to leader behaviors. *The Journal of Leadership Studies, 8*(1), 48–53.

Farling, M.L., Stone, G.A., & Winston, B.E. (1999). Servant leadership: Setting the stage for empirical research. *The Journal of Leadership Studies,* 49–55.

Feuerstein, A. (2000). School characteristics and parental involvement: Influences on participation in children's schools. *The Journal of Educational Research, 94*(1), 29–42.

Goertz, J. (2000). Creativity: An essential component for leadership in today's schools. *The Reoper Review, 22*(3), 158.

Goldberg, M. (2001). Leadership in education: Five commonalities. *Phi Delta Kappan, (82)*10, 757–762.

Harry, B. (1992). Restructuring the participation of African-American parents in special education. *Teaching Exceptional Children,* (January), 123–131.

Hoyle, J.R., & Slater, R.O. (2001). Love, happiness, and America's schools: The role of educational leadership in the 21st century. *Phi Delta Kappan, 82*(10), 790–794.

Lawrence-Lightfoot, S. (2003). *The essential conversation: What parents and teachers can learn from each other.* New York: Random House.

Lloyd, G.M. (1996). Family diversity, intellectual inequality, and academic achievement among American children. In A. Booth & J. Dunn (Eds.), *Family-school links: How do they affect educational outcomes?* (pp. 265–273). Mahwah, NJ: Erlbaum.

Martin, M.M. (1998). Trust leadership. *Journal of Leadership Studies, 5*(3), 41–49.

Montgomery, W. (2001). Creating culturally responsive inclusive classrooms. *Teaching Exceptional Children, 33*(4), 4.

National Association for Educating Young Children. (1996). NAEYC Position statement: Responding to linguistic and cultural diversity—recommendations for effective early childhood education. *Young Children,* January.

Pipho, C. (1994). Parental support for education. *Phi Delta Kappan, 76*(4), 270.

Shepard, R., & Rose, H. (1995). The power of parents: An empowerment model for increasing parent involvement in schools. *Education, 115*(3), 373.

Swap, S.M. (1993). *Developing home-school partnerships: From concept to practice.* New York: Teachers College Press.

Villa, C. (2003). Community building to serve all students. *Education, 123*(4), 777.

ACTIVITIES FOR EDUCATORS IN LEADERSHIP PREPARATION

1. Invite a Board of Education member, a parent volunteer, or the editor of the local newspaper to discuss community relations and school-community issues.

2. With anonymous IEPs, role play a Committee of Special Education meeting using three different scenarios focused on three different types of disability. Assign rotating roles to class participants. Following the role play, analyze the different perspectives of the meeting members and how issues were or were not resolved in each case. What changes could have helped the content and results of the meeting?

3. Develop a panel of parents to discuss issues relating to home-school connections, parent teacher conferences, and their aspirations for their local schools and their children. On one panel or by way of separate panels, invite parents from the elementary, middle, and secondary grade levels.

4. Have classmates write and share "administrator autobiographies" touching on issues such as early experiences with their school leaders, their feelings about authority, their convictions regarding the connections to community, and the paths that led them to become administrators.

5. Brainstorm the class's vision for the ideal school. What would be taught? How? By whom? How would the school be in relation to the community that it serves?

6. Examine popular magazines for images and articles for parents, families, mothers, and working women (such as Parenting, Family Circle, Good Housekeeping, etc.) and magazines for people of color and of different ethnic origins. What issues do these magazines address? From what perspective are they created? How do their audiences differ? How can they provide insights into families and how they live or hope to live?

7. Interview five friends or neighbors outside the business of education regarding their feelings about school, families, and the relationships

of school and community. Create a graphic organizer, a play, a choral reading, a poster presentation, a song ore another representation of some of the ideas you encountered.

8. Interview a principal at a local elementary, middle, or high school about issues of connection to family. Collect and discuss the interviews as a class to discover how family and community relations impact student learning. How and why do family and community relations differ at different developmental stages. How are these stages similar?

9. Select a local school district to analyze. Divide the class into two person teams to interview parents, students, custodians, bus drivers, business operators, retirees, local law enforcement, and other community members about their school. Focus on the relationship of the community to the school and vice versa. Combine the results to create a district community profile. Present the results of your study to the superintendent and to school authorities.

10. Using Patricia Schmidt's "ABCs of Cultural Understanding," study the cultural backgrounds of members of the class. Present your changes in thinking and your reflections as a result of discovering yours and others cultural backgrounds.

AFTERWORD

Culturally Relevant
or Culturally Responsive Pedagogy

Patricia Ruggiano Schmidt
Literacy Professor—Le Moyne College

Present and future educators who read this document will have taken an important first step in understanding how to engage families and communities for students' academic, social, and emotional development. So what's the next step?

I propose that educators who are prepared to engage parents are educators who can implement culturally relevant or culturally responsive pedagogy (Ladson-Billings, 1995; Au, 1993). Culturally relevant or culturally responsive pedagogy are terms coined by Gloria Ladsen-Billings in her book entitled *The Dreamkeepers* (1994) and Katherine Au, in her 1981 study of Hawaiian children and their teachers. Ladson-Billings recorded the work of eight successful teachers in urban settings. They had different teaching styles and were from African-American and European-American backgrounds, but they were similar in their connections and communication with the families and communities of their children. Au's study (1981) demonstrated that when teachers made literacy materials relevant to Hawaiian children, their literacy development significantly improved. Both Au and Ladson-Billings discovered teachers who could make connections

Preparing Educators to Communicate and Connect with Families and Communities, pages 77–82
Copyright © 2005 by Information Age Publishing
All rights of reproduction in any form reserved.

to the school culture, state-mandated curricula, and the children's homes and communities.

Educators who are prepared to engage families would also be prepared to implement culturally relevant or culturally responsive pedagogy. They would have examples of culturally relevant lessons at all grade levels and be able to view videos of those lessons. They would be mentored and supported by colleagues, administrators, and teacher educators as they created and implemented lessons and reached out to families and communities. Recently, studies from urban New York State schools demonstrate the following characteristics for successful culturally relevant pedagogy (Osborne, 1996; Schmidt, 2003):

1. positive relationships with families and community;
2. cultural sensitivity-reshaped curriculum, mediated for culturally valued knowledge;
3. high expectations;
4. active teaching methods;
5. teacher as facilitator;
6. student control of portions of the lesson—lots of talk —"healthy hum;" and
7. instruction around group and pairs—low anxiety.

With these characteristics internalized, educators would have the dispositions and abilities to engage and empower diverse families and communities to contribute to their children's academic and social development, thus leading us back to the common sense adage, "It takes a village to raise the child."

When analyzing the five sections in this document, it seemed obvious that each one related to the village raising the child and to culturally relevant or culturally responsive pedagogy. These sections actually explain the key ingredients for culturally relevant or culturally responsive pedagogy. They discuss ways teachers communicate and respond to families; ways to ascertain or influence teacher disposition to family engagement; ways teachers incorporate cultural and social contributions of family into schools; ways teachers empower families to interact with schools as collaborators in the educational process; and finally, ways educational leaders can make a difference in the whole process.

First, Friedman's section demonstrates the significance of miscommunication and the significance of carefully attentive communication. She makes us think about the importance of perceptions and perspectives. James Banks, in his article entitled, *The canon debate, knowledge construction, and multicultural education* (1993), establishes a framework for looking at differing perspectives in our nation's history. He talks about the need for transformative education and how it occurs when the academic disciplines are learned through the differing perspectives and contributions in the development of a content area. He suggests that in order to gain truth, one must attempt to understand as many perspectives as possible in a given situation.

As a result, to be multicultural and closer to truth in a discipline, one must develop compassion and try to walk in another's perspective shoes. For example, we need to understand the Columbus story and its perspectives, as well as the stories of the indigenous peoples of the Caribbean and their perspectives. Therefore, educators must attempt to understand and appreciate family and community perspectives in order to communicate effectively with families and communities of their students.

Tracy Knight Lackey helps us understand ways to change dispositions, so educators may begin to understand and appreciate varying perspectives in their classrooms and schools. Lackey's section emphasizes teacher disposition and changes in attitudes for community-family-school communication that enhance learning and teaching. She presents hopeful research and scenarios that might actually produce change.

Similarly, during the last two years, Schmidt (2003) has systematically worked with teachers in the development of culturally relevant pedagogy through changes in disposition and influences upon disposition. She surveyed teachers at the beginning of a volunteer in-service program and discovered that most thought they were doing a very good job of communicating with families. They also thought they knew a great deal about the community in which they taught. At the end of the first year, using the same survey, teachers expressed the fact that they had learned a great deal about the community and had begun to communicate in many more effective ways with parents. They met and talked to family members three times more the second semester of their in-service. Because they believed they had changed their attitudes about home-school-community collaboration, they created many culturally relevant lessons using parents and community members as primary sources in their units of study.

Family members visited classes to present first-hand experiences and actually taught about their occupations and interests. A mother brought in her newborn child for the unit on human development, a father talked about his own smoking habits for the unit on the respiratory system, and a grandmother told her favorite bedtime story for the folktale unit.

Multicultural literature, parents' occupations and avocations, and community leaders became important components of the curriculum. Students seemed to see the relevance in learning important aspects of the curriculum. In these cases, teachers' dispositions appeared to be influenced by in-service preparation around the *ABC's of Cultural Understanding and Commu-*

nication (Schmidt, 2001), a model mentioned in Friedmann's, Chernoff's, and Fenlon's sections. The teachers also received generous and consistent follow-up support from colleagues, administrators, and professors. They were mentored during the next year, and the school district actually paid expenses for their attendance and presentations of their teaching and learning at an international conference. Similar to the exhortations made in Chernoff's section, these European-American teachers in an urban setting seriously sought diverse cultural contributions from families and community resources.

Chernoff's section tells us specifically about culturally relevant or culturally responsive pedagogy without using the term. She explains how crucial it is to include the contributions of diverse cultures by linking them to the mental readiness needed for learning. The idea of drawing upon schema or prior knowledge and making connections between the known and the new are well established in the educational community, so it is only logical that when drawing upon cultural and social knowledge of diverse groups, educators are connecting with prior knowledge and experiences.

Luis Moll (1992) has completed research on the need to make use of cultural capital or "funds of knowledge." He believes that certain groups of people have aptitudes or abilities in areas that go unrecognized in schools. Educators must make connections with this cultural knowledge if students are to perform at potential levels. He discusses the oral story-telling abilities, musical abilities, spatial-relational abilities, and mechanical abilities as specific to certain groups. Culturally relevant pedagogy seems to be the right direction and does seem to explore power issues related to critical literacy. These power issues are addressed with great sensitivity in Fenlon's work for this document.

Fenlon's section deals directly with critical literacy when she explores the multiple means for preparing educators to empower families for their children's academic and social development. Similar to Edward's work in *A Path to Follow: Learning to Listen to Parents* (1999), we are reminded that parents are children's first teachers. Families know a lot about their children and that knowledge can facilitate teaching and learning. But since many parents are intimidated by the school setting, it is often difficult to get the information we need to prepare the proper program for a student. Edwards recommends parent interviews on neutral ground and encourages educators to take the time to do this. The time and effort are well worth it. If a teacher pursues parent meetings at the beginning of the year or before school is in session, she or he can establish a positive base for the entire year. These early efforts pay off during the school year and establish a strong working relationship. Both Fenlon and Edwards believe that the playing field needs to be equal for the respect needed for sharing and caring. Teachers know a lot about teaching and learning, but parents know much more about their children.

Kozik explores power and parental knowledge when he presents the memorable vignette that serves as the focusing event for his section. He explains the importance of educational leadership and gives us the necessary ingredients for the synchronization of village efforts. His touching vignette, supported by research throughout the section, seems to embrace the major aspects of the previous sections and promotes culturally relevant pedagogy. He reminds us that effective schools have effective leaders, who are compassionate, knowledgeable, trustworthy, and willing to reach out to level the field for meaningful dialogue. These leaders are change agents who make a difference.

Finally, in The *Epilogue*, two parents, Diane Heller and Marybeth Schillace provide testimonials to the significance of communicating and connecting with home and school for developing relationships with families and bringing relevant inclusive education that benefits all students. They believe that teacher and parent advocates provide the power to empower…and teachers and parents who work together to blur the boundaries between home and school can make great education for our children.

Furthermore, a wealth of information related to this document resides in appendices that serve as a resource for schools that adapt this document's framework for family-community empowerment and engagement in the education process. These resources will help districts and teacher education programs meet state mandates that are emerging throughout the nation.

New York State and many more states in our country are beginning to require that teacher certification programs prepare their graduates for family engagement. Additionally, research demonstrates the connection between academic achievement and family engagement. Finally, common sense and intuition proclaim that it takes a village to raise a child. Therefore, the purpose of this document, prepared by parents, teachers, teacher educators, and administrators is to assist present and future teachers in this important work. So we urge you with a statement from the heart of our belief systems, "Engagement of schools, families, and communities for our children's education marries us to a productive and powerful future. So let's get started now!"

REFERENCES

Au, K. (1993). *Literacy instruction in multicultural settings*. New York: Harcourt, Brace Javanovich College Publishers.

Au, K. & Mason, J. (1981). Social organization factors in learning to read. *Reading Research Quarterly, 17*(1), 115–152.

Banks, J. A. (1993). The canon debate, knowledge construction, and multicultural education. *Educational Researcher, 22*(5), 4–14.

Edwards, P.A., Pleasants, H., & Franklin, S. (1999). *A path to follow: Learning to listen to parents.* Portsmouth, NH: Heinemann.

Ladson-Billings, G. (1994). *The dreamkeepers: Successful teachers of African American children.* San Francisco, CA: Jossey-Bass.

Ladson-Billings, G. (1995). Culturally relevant teaching. *Research Journal, 32*(3), 465–491.

Moll, L.C. (1992). Bilingual classroom studies and community analysis: Recent trends. *Educational Researcher, 21*(2), 20–24. *Teacher Education, 9*(1), 27–39.

Osborne, A. B. (1996). Practice into theory into practice: Culturally relevant pedagogy for students we have marginalized and normalized. *Anthropology and Education Quarterly, 27*(3), 285–314.

Schmidt, P.R. (2001). The power to empower. In P.R. Schmidt and P.B. Mosenthal (Eds.), *Reconceptualizing literacy in the new age of multiculturalism and pluralism.* Greenwich, CT: Information Age Press.

Schmidt, P. R. (2003, December). *Culturally relevant pedagogy: A study of successful inservice.* Paper presented at the annual meeting of the National Reading Conference, Scottsdale, AZ.

EPILOGUE

Final Words—Part I

Diane Heller
Parent—Syracuse City School District

I've been lucky. My sons are 12 and 9, and since they began nursery school at age 3, all of their teachers have generally treated me as a peer. My sons' teachers find me willing to like them from the start. I also respect the teaching profession and have both an innate and a learned belief in educators and schools. But what if I didn't have a trusting nature, had been taught by life not to trust others, not to trust people in authority? What would my relationship to school and teachers be then? What if school hadn't been easy, been rewarding, but rather arduous and lacerating to my self-confidence? What if school hadn't felt like a haven, but a minefield full of work that I didn't understand, and people who I felt didn't understand or care about me? What if the adults with whom I spent 6 or 8 hours a day seemed alien, their words and behaviors foreign and inexplicable to me? It's clear to see how this would affect my schoolwork as a child, and my relationship with the school "system" as a parent.

My younger son has a serious illness that requires 24-hour vigilance, 365 days a year. He appears fine, and mostly, is fine, but we can never let down our watchfulness. Sending him to school was scary. Would his teachers be constantly aware, with 20 or 30 other little ones to look after and teach?

Preparing Educators to Communicate and Connect with Families and Communities, pages 83–86

Would he be safe? On a field trip, would someone notice if he lagged behind, felt ill, lost consciousness? As wonderful as our teachers have been, my husband or I have gone on school field trips, because we know that there may not be a carefully considered plan for our son's care. (In fairness, I like to go on the trips because I enjoy the experiences.) Usually, we discover that the school nurse hasn't known that a trip was scheduled for a certain day, and therefore, could not make a plan available for his care. Consequently, it has been our experience that there is a lack of communication and planning between school and home, and within the school, even among well-meaning, competent adults.

Concerns like ours are multiplied each school year, each day, each hour, in every classroom. I think parents wonder,

- "Will the teacher respect the fact that my daughter wears a headscarf because of our religious beliefs?"
- "Does the teacher speak any Spanish?"
- "Will my child be left out because he doesn't speak much English?"
- "Does the teacher really understand how special my child who lives with autism really is, how much he can do?

Dear educators, you can never underestimate what you mean to a child—what you say; how you say it; your verbal and non-verbal speech; a word or a laugh dropped here or there (perhaps not meant to be heard, but heard nonetheless); a loving word; and a shared joke that buoys a child's soul. Children know a lot, much of the time more than adults let themselves realize. They know if you respect them and their families and culture; if you are just "politically correct" in your speech and behavior, but don't feel it in your heart. No matter their I.Q., children have an E.Q.(Emotional Intelligence) that knows. And so do their families.

As a parent, I had always assumed that teacher training automatically and universally included course work and practical experiences for cultural awareness and sensitivity. I always thought they were prepared in the ways and means necessary to relate to families and engage them in the education process of their children. Generally speaking, I thought educators and administrators wanted parents and families involved in the school experience as much as possible.

At my children's school, the majority of the points addressed in this document are apparent. Parents are welcomed at any time to visit and to help. There is an "open-door" policy (with provision for student and staff safety); parents are encouraged to help in the classroom, as well as at special events. The curricula includes references to many cultures, including ones predominant in the school population, mainly African-American and Hispanic, and the principal and vice-principal have always been visible and accessible to parents.

As our group discussed at our daylong meetings, and as I read contributors' work, I said to myself, "Check. Check. Check. Got it at our school." This is my experience, but could all families in our school respond similarly? In my years there, the PTO has been all white, even though at least half the school's population is African-American and Hispanic. Most of the volunteers seen are European American. But at school events, such as plays and concerts, the turnout is *all* American. The auditorium is packed and joyous! Our families care and are there.

I see administrators and teachers who make the effort to include everyone in countless ways. I see teachers who are openly loving and caring, even the ones who are seen as tough and strict. I see work in the classrooms and bulletin boards, in the school library, in the display cases that reflect the panorama that is our school. But there is always room for improvement, so that all are included every day.

In this work, I've read wonderful ideas and practical suggestions for classrooms and schools. It is rich in resources for theoretical exploration, research, and everyday use. But it all comes back to you, the classroom teacher. We're waiting, we're ready, even those of us who don't seem to be. Open your doors to us, and show us how to help you.

Final Words—Part II

Marybeth A. Schillace
Parent

I have maintained a major hope throughout the idea-generating, creation, and promotion of this book. My hope is that the incredibly passionate discussions that we have had as a team will translate into passionate action by those who read the pages of this book...action that will benefit every student, parent, and educator in our educational system.

As the parent of a child who has special needs, an educator, and a member of the team who authored this book, I have had the privilege of viewing the subject of this book from three perspectives. First and foremost, my parental perspective was shaped by all that transpired during the course of our discussions. They provided me with a greater understanding and respect for the challenging situations that educators face as they deal with students and families. My teacher perspective prompted me to incorporate what I learned from our discussions into practice. My perspective as a member of the team made me want to be a life-long learner of family and community engagement. In this *Epilogue,* I want to focus on the words, advocate and advocacy.

My experiences as a parent have impressed upon me the importance of advocacy for every student in our educational system. Being an advocate is not an easy task. I know, since the process began for my husband and me with our child's first kindergarten IEP. We found the numerous meetings, the phone calls, the paperwork and the intense emotions tied to being our child's primary advocates was exhausting. In the midst of trying to secure our child's educational future, as well as preserve her individuality in her time of educational transition and beyond, we had all we could do to focus on enjoying the present. We believe more than ever that there must be an easier way to advocate and foster a mutual understanding of what we have dreamed for our child.

My husband and I knew, before negotiating our child's IEP, that particular schools and school districts exist that have reputations for being more inclusive than others. We knew that some districts have been proactive in paving the roads for inclusion, and have engaged in best practices relative to communicating with all students and their families. However, there are many districts that only react to inclusion in a minimal manner and appear to ignore the desperate needs of our ever-increasing, diverse student population and their families. Regardless of our fears, my husband and I have hoped to be welcomed as advocates for our child.

I consider myself an advocate, knowledgeable about the educational system. However, I know that there are some parents who are not so knowledgeable and may feel rather intimidated. It has always been my belief, that regardless of what type of an advocate an individual may be, those in the education profession should greet all families with the utmost respect...the type of respect that is so often spoken of in the character education programs within our schools ...mutual respect. With this notion of mutual respect in mind, I encourage all who read this book, to passionately practice the ideas and recognize the importance of advocacy.

HOME-TO-SCHOOL COMMUNICATION

The following checklists were taken from sources cited in the references and were developed as gentle reminders for you to consider. They cover three interrelated areas: parent conferences, written communication, and other ways to communicate with parents.

PARENT CONFERENCES

Good parent-teacher conferences do not simply happen. They are planned events, guided by common sense and the following practical principles.

- Set the conference at a mutually agreed-upon time; it is disrespectful to set the conference at a time convenient only to you.
- Plan what you will say, and prepare to share student work; it will communicate that you take this conference seriously.
- Take time to ease the parent into the conference; avoid rushing to make your points.
- Listen to what the parents have to say; they are the experts on their child's out-of-school behavior and demeanor. When you model listening, the parents are more likely to listen.
- Speak clearly and simply; avoid jargon. Many parents will pretend to understand when they are too embarrassed to have you explain a term.

Preparing Educators to Communicate and Connect with Families and Communities, pages 87–89
Copyright © 2005 by Information Age Publishing
All rights of reproduction in any form reserved.

- Consider that parents need time to digest information before acting, thus avoid insisting on coming to closure. Set a return date to revisit possible solutions.
- Thank the parents for their time, and express appreciation for their interest and cooperation.
- Avail yourself of the counsel of others; try out what you will say with a trusted colleague or supervisor.
- Select a space and setting that is comfortable and private; nothing works better to annoy parents than having to sit at a small desk with another parent seated three feet away.
- Invite a mediator if you anticipate a negative encounter; this helps to "cool down" the situation and reduce miscommunication.
- Select a point of focus for the conference, and avoid overwhelming parents with too much information.
- Send a follow-up thank you note or phone call to reinforce the parents' participation.
- Schedule the conference with a reasonable amount of time for parents to share information.

WRITTEN COMMUNICATION

There is writing and there is bad writing. Today, we are barraged with messages in all forms, and thus we are sensitive to what's received. The following tips are intended to help you keep your written communication simple and short.

- Notes sent home should contain a response section, so that parents feel they have a "say," not just the teacher or school. See Epstein's TIPS to parents on her website. Each communiqué gives the parents a chance to respond.
- Newsletters should include children's work or accomplishments, not just publicize school events or expectations.
- If possible, use e-mail to communicate quickly and efficiently with individual parents or entire classrooms.
- Let parents know at the beginning of the year how you plan to communicate in writing. Children are not the best daily messengers, thus parents need a "heads up" to be aware of notices and other forms of written communication.
- When at all possible, send communication in the home language of the students. Sometimes, parents can be your translators if your school doesn't have a paid translator.

OTHER WAYS TO COMMUNICATE WITH PARENTS

While parent conferences and written communication are primarily the ways we communicate with parents, there are other channels as well. We need to be aware that these collectively help to build effective ties between the home and school.

- Face-to-face contact at entry and exit times.
- Phone calls home to communicate celebrations as well as concerns.
- Publicizing open houses and school events to encourage parental engagement.
- Placing items in the local papers to increase interest in the school as the center of the community.
- Suggestion boxes in places of prominence to encourage parents to contribute ideas for improvement.
- Sending home activity kits for families to provide extensions of school activities.
- Individualized invitations to volunteer in classroom and school activities.

APPENDIX B

SAMPLE LETTER

Families of Children Receiving Special Education in Pre-school Who Are Eligible for Kindergarten in the Next Year

Dear Parent(s):

As you know, your pre-school child will soon be eligible for kindergarten in the Baldwinsville School District. The transition to kindergarten from pre-school can be an exciting and anxious time for children and families. If your child may require special services in kindergarten, your close involvement in planning their program is important to me.

I am writing this letter to you early in the year so that we might plan ahead for your child's entrance into kindergarten. Parents often have many questions about what their child's kindergarten experience will be like and how services such as special education, speech, and other therapies are delivered to the child. Please let this letter serve as an invitation to call me at the School District Office. I can begin to answer some of the questions that may be coming to mind, and can tell you about some of the ways that we can provide services in the district. Usually in the spring prior to the child entering kindergarten, I often take parents on visits to our elementary schools to observe classrooms and meet with school staff.

Preparing Educators to Communicate and Connect with Families and Communities, pages 91–92
Copyright © 2005 by Information Age Publishing

I look forward to meeting and talking with you about this important transition for your child. Working together we can plan a successful start to your child's school career.

Sincerely,

Amanda Fenlon, Ed.D.
Administrator for Pre-school Special Education

SAMPLE CALENDAR OF FAMILY INVOLVEMENT ACTIVITIES

August

Home visits
Family Center open 8 a.m. to 4 p.m.
Ongoing evaluation of activities

September

First day of school activities
Positive phone calls to all families
Parent-friendly letter/survey of volunteer interest sent home
Family Center open 8 a.m. to 4 p.m.
Open House—Ice Cream Social
Welcome folders sent to each new family
After-school workshop for teachers: Working with Culturally Diverse Families
    (parent facilitators)
Action team meeting
Family support group meeting
Ongoing evaluation of activities

October

Family Center open 8 a.m. to 4 p.m.
Dad/child Saturday breakfast
Bring your parents to school day
ESL classes for family members
Family science night
Welcome folders sent to each new family
Family education workshop: Positive
Parenting Strategies
Family support group meeting
Ongoing evaluation of activities

November

Family Center open 8 a.m. to 4 p.m.
Parent-teacher conferences (morning and evening)
Grandparents day
Family education workshop: Second Time Around Parenting for Grandparents
Welcome folders sent to each new family
Action team meeting
ESL classes for family members
Family math night
Family support group meeting
Ongoing evaluation of activities

December

Family Center open 8 a.m. to 4 p.m.
Welcome folders sent to each new family
Family education workshop: Monitoring Television/Computer Time
Family support group meeting
Ongoing evaluation of activities

January

Family Center open 8 a.m. to 4 p.m.
Welcome folders sent to each new family
Action team meeting
Family education workshop: Anger
Management
Family support group meeting
Ongoing evaluation of activities

February

Family Center open 8 a.m. to 4 p.m.
Family science night
GED classes for family members
Welcome folders sent to each new family
After-school workshop for teachers:
Working with Families Who Have Children with Disabilities (parent facilitators)
Family education workshop: Keeping
Children Safe from Abduction
Family support group meets

March

Family Center open 8 a.m. to 4 p.m.
Take your child to work day
Welcome folders sent to each new family
GED classes for family members
Family math night
Action team meeting
Family education workshop: Preventing
Substance Abuse
Family support group meeting
Ongoing evaluation of activities

April

Family Center open 8 a.m. to 4 p.m.
Mom/child Saturday breakfast
Welcome folders sent to each new family
Family education workshop: Effective
Communication with Teachers
International festival for families
Parent-teacher conferences (morning and evening)
Family support group meeting
Ongoing evaluation of activities

May

Family Center open 8 a.m. to 4 p.m.
Teacher appreciation week
Recognition awards for volunteers
Transition student/parent activities for graduating students
Welcome folders sent to each new family
Family education workshop: Summer Learning Activities for Families

Family support group meeting
Action team meeting
Ongoing evaluation of activities

June

Family Center open 8 a.m. to 4 p.m.
Action team meets to plan for coming year
Summative evaluation of year's activities

APPENDIX D

SAMPLE SYLLABI FOR IN-SERVICE AND PRE-SERVICE EDUCATION PROGRAMS

The following courses are among a growing number nationwide that prepare educators for school-family-community collaboration. The Harvard Family Research Project is also working with teachers' colleges and school districts to prepare teachers to work with parents. The project maintains a website of syllabi for teacher preparation courses in family involvement that may be accessed from: http://www.gse.harvard.edu/hfrp/projects/fine/resources/syllabus/index.html.

Nationwide, there is a growing recognition of the importance of training educators in school-family-community collaboration, although "in practice such training is not happening as widely or as quickly as necessary" (Kirschenbaum, 2001, p. 188). Surveys of higher education practices over the past two decades indicate that more institutions are incorporating family involvement into teacher preparation coursework, although only a minority of institutions offer a "comprehensive program in school-family-community relations that gives educators a thorough grounding in the theory, research and practice of partnerships" (Kirschenbaum, 2001, p. 188). An ongoing debate centers on whether colleges and universities should offer required courses in school-community-family involvement or "infuse the content throughout the curriculum," or both (Kirschenbaum, 2001, p. 194).

Preparing Educators to Communicate and Connect with Families and Communities, pages 97–101
Copyright © 2005 by Information Age Publishing

EDU 565 Home/School/Community Collaboration
Le Moyne College Education Department
Syracuse, New York

Due to changing demographics and definitions of family, the African proverb, "It takes a village to raise a child," has gained new emphasis in our society. As an important institution of the village, schools need to make strong connections with the village and its families. Also, research suggests that effective communication between home and school is critical to the academic development of all children and the creation of successful classrooms and schools (Heath, 1983; Mandel Morrow, 1996; Schmidt, 1999; Edwards, 1999, 2004).

Therefore, educators must become more aware of children's homes and communities and strengthen communication. Such ideas as culturally relevant pedagogy (Osborne, 1996) joinfostering (Faltis, 1993; Schmidt, 2000), conflict resolution (Katz & Lawyer, 1993), group process (Kormanski, 1999), community collaboration and consultation (Paloma McCaleb, 1994; Kampwirth, 1999), ABC's of Cultural Understanding and Communication (Schmidt, 1998, 2001), and parent stories (Edwards, 1999) have demonstrated the power of teachers, family, and community connections. The implementation of these plans or formulas has generally been successful, but there is little understanding of the person-to-person unstructured conversations between families and educators that develop the relationships necessary to foster home, school, and community connections. Therefore, the purpose of this course is to help teachers learn specific ways to blur the boundaries between home and school in order to develop community learning partnerships.

Family, Child, and Teacher Interaction in Regular and Inclusive Settings
Bank Street College of Education
New York City, New York

Rena Rice has taught the Family, Child and Teacher Interaction in a Regular and Inclusive Settings graduate course at the Bank Street College of Education since 1990, although the college has offered a course in school-family relations for the past 50 years (Kirschenbaum, 2001). The class focuses on developing competency in school-family relations, building content knowledge and skills, and changing attitudes, with emphasis on the latter. The experiences students undergo during the class help them to "look at families in different ways" than when they began the course. "School-family relations is an area that all teachers have anxiety about," Ms. Rice indicated, "even experienced teachers. It should be a part of all education classes" (personal communication, August 13, 2002).

Beyond the traditional teaching methods found in most college classes, Ms. Rice introduces a variety of strategies to help her students learn more about families of diverse backgrounds and develop empathy and understanding for their perspectives. These include role-playing, self-reflection, modeling, and interactive learning methods.

Assignments include students interviewing a parent of different socioeconomic and/or ethnic background from their own about their feelings and experiences concerning school-family relations, analyzing and critiquing family involvement policies and practices utilizing the National PTA Standards (1977), and developing plans to include parents in a curriculum study. These activities help move students beyond the "myth of physical availability" that assumes parents cannot be actively involved in their children's education unless they are present in the classroom.

Ms. Rice views her students as teachers who will be "agents of change" in their respective schools. She is hopeful that the class will motivate students to change school policies from ones that often "distance families" into ones that welcome and encourage greater family involvement and improved school-family relations (personal communication, August 13, 2002).

Leadership for School, Family, and Community Collaboration
Le Moyne College Education Department
Syracuse, New York

The purpose of this course is to present educational leaders with numerous opportunities to study new information and refine known information concerning collaboration. They will be practicing both types in and out of the college classroom. This course is required for graduate education students preparing to become school administrators and change agents—leaders who see the need to reach out and engage families and community members for the education of our young people.

Research strongly suggests that blurring the boundaries between schools and families and schools and communities is an essential element for the successful education of our young people (Boykin, 1976; Heath, 1983; Epstein, 1988; Trueba, Jacobs & Kirton, 1990; Schmidt, 2000; Edwards, 2004). Therefore, in this course, we will survey models and approaches for schools, families, and community collaboration and examine theoretical models, socio-political issues, and practical ideas related to collaboration. Resource people from schools and community will visit the college classroom to share their knowledge and experiences, and graduate students will interview school, community, and family members to discover their understandings of collaboration for children's education. Course objectives are:

- To develop an understanding of the importance of home-school-community collaboration;

- To analyze the historical and current relationships between families, schools, and communities;
- To develop an understanding and appreciation of diverse societal influences that affect families and to develop an understanding of diverse populations;
- To examine theoretical perspectives and professional practices related to family-school-community relationships;
- To demonstrate a variety of skills and abilities in communicating with families;
- To develop an understanding of the importance of home-school-community collaboration;
- To analyze the historical and current relationships between families, schools, and communities;
- To develop an understanding and appreciation of diverse societal influences that affect families and to develop an understanding of diverse populations;
- To examine theoretical perspectives and professional practices related to family-school-community relationships;
- To demonstrate a variety of skills and abilities in communicating with families;
- To demonstrate the ability to plan and implement in-service activities that promote home-school-community collaboration; and
- To demonstrate knowledge of programs, resources, and support groups for families, teachers, and children.

School, Family, and Community Relations Course
University of Rochester
Rochester, New York

School, Family, and Community Relations is a required course for graduate students earning masters degrees in school administration at the Warner Graduate School of Education and Human Development. The course, taught by Dr. Howard Kirschenbaum for the past seven years, introduces administrators, teachers, and counselors to "the dramatic changes taking place in school, family, and community relations" (Kirschenbaum, 2001, p. 1). Students survey "a wide variety of models and approaches taking place today for uniting schools, parents, and community institutions into meaningful partnerships for academic success and healthy development of young people" (Kirschenbaum, 2001, p. 1). Students also examine "the many theoretical, political, and practical issues associated with these new models of collaboration" (Kirschenbaum, 2001, p. 1).

Because he works closely with the Rochester City School District on research and implementation projects involving family involvement, including assisting in developing the district's strategic plan for parent involvement, Dr. Kirschenbaum is able to bring his own experiences into the classroom. He also invites resource people from the school and community into the classroom, including active parent volunteers, and takes the class on field trips into the community. Students are also required to go out into the community and conduct school case studies by interviewing parents, teachers, and administrators, and gathering information about schools previously unfamiliar to them (Kirschenbaum, 2001). "It's a lot to cover in one course," said Dr. Kirschenbaum, "but I think it's possible to give students a good feel for the newer 'partnership paradigm' in education and some of the theory, research, and practice associated with it" (personal communication, August 19, 2002).

Topics covered in the course include:

- School-family communication;
- Partnership models;
- Parent involvement at school;
- Measuring and evaluating parent involvement;
- Parent empowerment;
- Parent rights, school choice, and related controversial issues;
- School-linked services;
- Community support for schools;
- Tutoring and mentoring;
- School-to-work programs;
- Service learning;
- School-linked services; and
- Issues and controversies in school-community relations.

APPENDIX E

POLICIES

Over the past decade, increasing attention has been given to the growing body of evidence demonstrating the positive impact of school-family-community collaborations. At the same time, there is recognition of a "serious discrepancy" between pre-service preparation of teachers and the types of family involvement activities that teachers are increasingly expected to perform (Shartrand, Weiss, & Lopez, 1997). Until recently, most state certification departments did not require courses on family involvement for pre-service educators. Since the late 1990's, the number of states requiring that teachers have knowledge and skills related to parent and community involvement has increased significantly, and many states have begun to mandate pre-service training and ongoing professional development in family involvement and school-family-community partnerships (Kirschenbaum, 2001; Hiatt-Michael, 2001; Gray, 2001). However, California is the only state thus far that has enacted legislation mandating pre-service and practicing teachers "to serve as active partners with parents and guardians in the education of children" (California Education Code 44291.2, 1993).

The New York State Education Department (New York State, 2001) requires all teachers receiving certification by 2004 to have training that covers:

- The impact of…factors in the home, school, and community on students' readiness to learn (p. 12);
- The importance of productive relationships and interactions among the school, home, and community for enhancing student learning— and skill in fostering effective relationships and interactions to support student growth and learning (p. 65);

Preparing Educators to Communicate and Connect with Families and Communities, pages 103–105
103

- Experiences practicing skills for interacting with parents and caregivers (p. 15);
- Participating in collaborative partnerships for the benefit of students with disabilities, including family-strengthening partnerships (p. 41); and
- Communicating assessment results to parents, caregivers, and school personnel (p. 58).

Additionally, New York's eight Standards for Teachers includes one standard that specifically addresses family involvement:

The teacher promotes parental involvement and collaborates effectively with other staff, the community, higher education, other agencies, and cultural institutions, as well as parents and other caregivers, for the benefit of students. (New York State, 1998)

The Massachusetts State Department of Education's Parent, Family, and Community Involvement Guide (2000) recommends that training in family-school-community involvement for both pre-service and practicing teachers include:

- Research findings and information on the benefits of family involvement;
- Strategies for helping educators "develop the skills, sensitivity, and insight necessary to work effectively with parents representing a variety of family structures and cultural backgrounds;"
- Strategies for helping school staff to create a welcoming school environment;
- Methods of developing "effective parent outreach and engagement strategies, including the…regular two-way communication between the school and home;"
- Strategies to overcome barriers to family involvement;
- Development of effective communication skills;
- Models of successful school, family, and community partnerships and methods of building these partnerships;
- Community resources and programs and strategies for connecting families with these resources; and
- Opportunities for staff, families, and community members to come together to learn skills in leadership, collaboration, advocacy, and shared decision making. (Massachusetts Department of Education, 2000)

The Council for Exceptional Children (2000) recommends three core knowledge and five skills that new teachers need to be able to work effectively with families. As teachers utilize these knowledge and skills to establish relationships with families, they will create bonds and establish dialogues based upon mutual respect for the shared responsibility of educating children. The National Board for Professional Teaching Standards includes parent involvement among 11 generalist standards for educators (Hiatt-Michael, 2001).

APPENDIX F

PRACTICES

The *New Skills for Schools,* (Shartrand, Weiss, and Lopez, 1997) offers a comprehensive framework that "illustrates the range of training for family involvement" to prepare teachers.

Family Involvement Framework for Teacher Training

Type	Goals
General Family Involvement	To provide general information on the goals of, benefits of, and barriers to family involvement. To promote knowledge of, skills in, and positive attitudes toward involving parents.
General Family Knowledge	To promote knowledge of different families' cultural beliefs, childrearing practices, structures, and living environments. To promote an awareness of and respect for different backgrounds and lifestyles.
Home-School Communication	To provide techniques and strategies to improve two-way communication between home and school (and/or parent and teacher).
Family Involvement in Learning Activities	To provide information on how to involve parents in their children's learning outside of the classroom.
Families Supporting Schools	To provide information on ways to involve parents in helping the school, both within and outside the classroom.

Family Involvement Framework for Teacher Training (Cont.)

Type	Goals
Schools Supporting Families	To examine how schools can support families' social, educational, and social service needs through parent education programs, parent centers, and referrals to other community or social services.
Families as Change Agents	To introduce ways to support and involve parents and families in decision making, action research, child advocacy, parent and teacher training, and development of policy, programs, and curriculum.

Maintaining that "no one method of instruction can prepare teachers to work effectively with families and communities," Shartrand, Weiss, and Lopez (1997) advocate for approaches that are "comprehensive, integrated, and varied." Best practices that they recommend include "providing prospective teachers with opportunities to develop problem-solving skills by exposing them to challenging situations that require them to negotiate sensitive issues," and having them work in schools and communities under the guidance of experienced professionals, apply research skills for a better understanding of families and communities, and utilize information to develop family involvement activities.

Among the nine recommendations made by the New Skills for New Teachers study (1997), five directly address school-family-community collaborations:

1. Make training available to elementary, middle, and high school teachers; early childhood educators receive more pre-service training than other teachers;

2. Improve the effectiveness of training through collaboration across subspecialties and disciplines—health and social services;

3. Integrate training throughout teacher preparation curriculum rather than treating it as an isolated component;

4. Sustain teachers' knowledge, skills, and positive attitudes toward families through in-service training; and

5. Move beyond classroom-based teaching methods by offering teachers direct field experiences working with families.

Continual professional development for teachers is needed as family structures continue to change, requiring "new or different family outreach strategies from what may have been effective in the past" (U.S. Department of Education, 1997). These trainings may include topics such as strategies for contacting parents, students' home culture, appreciation of diversity, effective communication, conflict resolution, team building, and ways to involve parents as leaders and decision makers in the school. In addition, as more children with disabilities are included in the general education curriculum, both special and regular educators will need training that focuses on effectively interacting with parents of children with disabilities to involve them as equal partners in the educational planning and decision making process for their child (Garriott, Wandry, & Snyder, 2000).

In addressing issues related to poverty, professional development for educators needs to shift away from mothers of poverty as contributors to the problem of underachieving students, to focusing on "how the schools, as powerful institutions of social control, reproduce inequalities of social class and stereotypes of the poor" (Bloom, 2001) and "socialize children into a white, middle-class system," promoting values which may be in opposition to the values of some families in the school (Donn & Konzal, 2002, p. 28). Possible topics for discussion include poverty and privilege, stereotyping, maternal suspicion, and unrealistic middle class expectations for families living in poverty.

PARENTS AS TEACHERS

Parents of different cultures, including Native Americans, Hispanic, Asian, and others can take an active role in presenting parental perspectives in professional development opportunities for teachers that focus on family involvement. In California, "mentor parents" provide professional development to school staff on parent involvement and home-school communication. One workshop addressed obstacles to parent involvement in schools, including parents' negative past experiences that discourage participation, and perceived teacher biases based on parents' different socioeconomic status, race, gender, physical appearance, or language ability (U.S. Department of Education, Family Involvement, 1997).

Reading at Home is a course taught by parents to parents of K–3 students in several Illinois Solid Foundation schools. The course helps parents encourage children to develop a lifelong love of reading. Parents who take the course attend three weekly, 90-minute sessions that are taught in groups of ten and led by parents trained as group leaders. Parents learn activities and exercises to do with their children and then share experiences with the group. Many of the activities require no previous planning or extra supplies. In several schools where students speak more than one language, parent volunteers are translating the course into multiple languages. (Reading at Home, 2001)

PARENTS AS FACULTY

Parents have also been effectively utilized as co-instructors in the professional development of teachers. The Family as Faculty project begun in 1999 at the University of South Florida recruits family members as guest lecturers in education classes with the goal of enhancing "home-school partnerships by providing future educators with opportunities to listen to the voices of families from a variety of walks of life" (Family as Faculty, 2000). Topics presented by parents have included attention deficit disorder, language barriers, socioeconomic barriers, teacher conferences, and grandparent caregiving, according to project director Dr. Jane Sergay. One parent of a child with a learning disability shared with the students a strategy of videotaping interactions with her daughter to help the teacher relate more effectively with her. Some parents have brought their children to classes. Other parents have agreed to role-play with students in counseling education courses.

Parents recruited for the program are provided a three-day orientation and training during which they reflect on their experiences, identify specific issues and personal stories, and consider what makes a good presentation. They also give practice presentations and give one another feedback. Parents receive a training stipend and fee for each presentation. This program is now being replicated in other institutions, including the University of North Carolina and the University of Central Florida.

The Division for Early Childhood of the Council for Exceptional Children (Stayton & Miller, 1993) recommends that family members be involved in planning, implementing, and evaluating pre-service curriculum as well as in delivering in-service training. Although the approaches to co-instruction vary in degree and content, the emphasis is still on the ability of family members to share their personal experiences and perspectives from living with a child with a disability with professionals. "This ability to understand the world from the perspective of family members is critical to providing educational services to children and families that reflect a family-centered philosophy" (Fuller & Olsen, 1998, p. 176).

APPENDIX G

EVALUATION

As schools implement new practices in family involvement, the benefits for students, parents, staff, school, and community need to be evaluated on an ongoing basis (Epstein, Coates, Salinas, Sanders & Simon, 1997; Funk-houser & Gonzales, 1997). Surveys of family, school staff, and community participation in, and satisfaction with, family involvement activities, interviews, sign-in sheets for parent volunteers, and comparisons of "before and after" practices may be used to assess the effectiveness of practices. Whether these evaluations are formal or informal, "it is important to learn how each practice is working to inform future plans and improvements" (Epstein et. al, 1997, p. 30). Schools should remain open to suggestions from parents about how their involvement can be improved (Rosenthal & Sawyers, 1996). Family coordinators should take a lead role in coordinating evaluation activities.

The following is a list of evaluation instruments that may be utilized to assess the benefits of family involvement practices and school-home-community practices.

FAMILY INVOLVEMENT EVALUATION INSTRUMENTS

- Appendix F: Schools That Say "Welcome" (Wisconsin Department of Public Instruction, 1996).
- Checklist for a Welcoming First Impression of Your School (The National Association of Elementary School Principals, 2001, pp. 51–52).

Preparing Educators to Communicate and Connect with Families and Communities, pages 111–113
Copyright © 2005 by Information Age Publishing
All rights of reproduction in any form reserved.

- Checklist for Improving Parental Involvement (Jesse, 1995).
- Checklist of Quality Indicators of the Six National Standards for Parent/Family Involvement (Available in English, Chinese, Cambodian, Korean, Spanish, and Vietnamese); (Christenson & Sheridan, 2001, pp. 210–214; National PTA, 1999).
- Educator Reflection: Gathering Perceptions and Collaborating on Results (Blank & Kershaw, 1998).
- End-of-Year Evaluation: School-Family-Community Partnerships (Epstein, Coates, Salinas, Sanders, & Simon, 1997, pp. 137–143).
- Evaluating PTA Parent/Family Involvement Activities (National PTA, Building Successful Partnerships, 2000, p. 222).
- Evaluating Group Process (National PTA, Building Successful Partnerships, 2000, pp. 215–216).
- Faculty Survey (National PTA, Building Successful Partnerships, 2000, pp. 211–212).
- Father-Friendliness Organizational Self-Assessment and Planning Tool for Early Childhood Education Programs (National Head Start Association, 2002).
- How Welcome Are Parents in Our School? (National Parent Teacher Association, 1990; North Central Regional Educational Laboratory, Questionnaire, 1996).
- Inventory for Creating School-Family Connections (Christenson & Sheridan, 2001, pp. 223–227).
- Inventory of Present Practices of School-Family-Community Partnerships (Epstein, Coates, Salinas, Sanders, & Simon, 1997, pp. 122–125).
- Parent Involvement in Our Schools (National PTA, Building Successful Partnerships, 2000, pp. 201–204).
- Parent Involvement Inventory (Illinois State Board of Education, 1994; North Central Regional Educational Laboratory, Parent, 1996).
- Parent Survey (National PTA, Building Successful Partnerships, 2000, pp. 205–209).
- Resource 1–1: Survey on Parent Involvement (Dietz, 1997, pp. 7–12).
- Resource 1–2: Learning Together—A Checklist for Schools (Dietz, 1997, pp. 13–15).
- Resource 1–3: Decision-Making Table (Dietz, 1997, pp. 16–18).
- School-community self-assessment on community and parent engagement based on five community values (Fresno Unified Schools, 2002).
- Survey (self-study)—Home Involvement in Schooling (Mental Health in Schools Training and Technical Assistance Center, 1996).

- Taking Stock: Checklists for Self-Assessment (Henderson, Marburger & Ooms, 1986, pp. 79–93).
- Using the Model to Guide Parent Involvement Practice (Hornby, 2000, pp. 27–31).

SCHOOL–HOME–COMMUNITY EVALUATION INSTRUMENTS

- Building Community—Strengthening Partnerships: Parent Survey (Blank & Kershaw, 1998, pp. 25–27).
- Checklist of Quality Indicators of the Six National Standards for Parent/Family Involvement (Available in English, Chinese, Cambodian, Korean, Spanish, and Vietnamese); (Christenson & Sheridan, 2001, pp. 210–214; National PTA, Building Successful Partnerships, 1999).
- Community–School Partnership Assessment (Blank & Langford, 2000).
- Ideas into Practice, School–Community Partnerships: Self-Study Survey (Mental Health in Schools Training and Technical Assistance Center, 1999, p. 9).
- Parent Involvement Inventory (Illinois State Board of Education, 1994; North Central Regional Educational Laboratory, Parent, 1996).
- School–community self-assessment on community and parent engagement based on five community values (Fresno Unified Schools, 2002).
- Survey (Self-Study)—School–Community Partnerships (Mental Health in Schools Training and Technical Assistance Center, School–Community Partnerships, 1999).

APPENDIX H

CONTACTS AND RESOURCES

Academic Development Institute
> The Center for the School Community Family Study Institute
> Illinois Family Education Center
> 121 N. Kickapoo St.
> Lincoln, IL 62656
> Phone: (217) 732-6462
> Website: www.adi.org

Bank Street College of Education
> Ms. Rena Rice
> 610 West 112th Street
> New York, NY 10025
> Phone: (212) 875-4508
> E-mail: renarice@bankstreet.edu

Buffalo Parent Center
> Bonnie Nelson, Supervisor
> Buffalo Board of Education
> 15 E. Genesee Street
> Buffalo, NY 14203
> (716) 851-3651 or 3652

Buffalo Public School #45
> Colleen Carota, Principal
> 141 Hoyt
> Buffalo, NY 14213
> Phone: (716) 888-7077

Preparing Educators to Communicate and Connect with Families and Communities, pages 115–123
Copyright © 2005 by Information Age Publishing

BUILD Academy
Mary Kay Muscarella
Technology Integration Specialist
340 Fougeron St.
Buffalo, NY 14211
Phone: (716) 897-8110

Center on School, Family and Community Partnerships
Johns Hopkins University
3505 North Charles Street
Baltimore, MD 21218
Phone: (410) 518-8800
Website: http://www.csos.jhu.edu/p2000/center.htm

Center Without Walls
Resources for Children with Special Needs, Inc.
116 East 16th Street, 5th Floor
New York, NY 10003
Phone: (212) 677-4650
E-mail: info@resourcesntc.org
Website: www.resourcesnyc.org

Children's Aid Society
Richard Negron
102 East 22nd St.
New York, NY 10010
Phone: (212) 254-4587
E-mail: Richard@childrensaidsociety.org
Website: http://www.childrensaid.net

Coalition for Community Schools
c/o Institute for Educational Leadership
1001 Connecticut Ave., NW Suite 310
Washington, DC 20036
Phone: (202) 822-8405
E-mail: ccs@iel.org

Commonwealth Institute for Parent Leadership
Beverly N. Raimondo, Director
Prichard Committee for Academic Excellence
Lexington, KY
Phone: (859) 233-9849 or (800) 928-2111
Website: http://www.cipl.org/index.html

Community School District #10
    Mario Fico, Director of Information Technology
    One Fordham Plaza
    Bronx, NY 10458
    Phone: (718) 329-8064
    Website: http://www.csd10.org/

Family Friendly Schools
    13080 Brookmead Drive
    Manassas, VA 20112
    Phone: (800) 648-6082
    Website: www.Familyfriendlyschools.org

Family Involvement Network of Educators
    Harvard Family Research Project
    Longfellow Hall
    Appian Way
    Cambridge, MA 02138
    Phone: (617) 495-9108
    Website: http://www.gse.harvard.edu/hfrp/projects/fine/resources/
            syllabus/index.html

The Fatherhood Project/Families and Work Institute
    267 Fifth Avenue, 2nd Floor
    New York, NY 10016
    Phone: (212) 465-2044
    E-mail: jlevine@familiesandwork.org
    Website: www.fatherhoodproject.org

Fathers Network
    11620 NE Eighth St.
    Bellevue, WA 98008-3937
    Phone: (425) 747-4004, ext. 218
    E-mail: jmay@fathersnetwork.org
    Website: www.fathersnework.org/674.html

Fayetteville Elementary School
    Nancy Smith, Principal
    700 South Manlius Street
    Fayetteville, NY 13066
    Phone: (315) 682-1320
    E-mail: nsmith@fm.cnyric.org

First Day Foundation
    210 Main Street
    P.O. Box 10
    Bennington, Vermont 05201-0010
    Toll Free Phone: 1-877-FIRST DAY
    E-mail: firstday@sover.net
    Website: http://www.firstday.com/

14th Street–Union Square Local Development Corporation
    Michelle Jarney, Director of Education
    40 Irving Place
    New York City, NY 10003
    Phone: (212) 460-1200
    E-mail: JarneyM@coned.com

Federation of Families for Children's Mental Health Needs
    1101 King Street, Suite 420
    Alexandria, Virginia 22314
    Phone: (703) 684-7710
    Website: http://www.ffcmh.org/

Florida Partnership for Family Involvement in Education
    Jane Sergay, Director
    University of South Florida
    3500 E. Fletcher Ave., Suite 225
    Tampa, FL 33613
    Phone: (813) 558-5365
    E-mail: jsergay@tempest.coedu.usf.edu

Fresno Unified School District
    Parent Engagement Center
    2940 N. Blackstone
    Fresno, CA 93703
    Phone: (559) 241-7237
    Website: http://fresno.k12.ca.us/divdept/pec/

Greensville Public Schools
    Dr. Margaret Lee
    Title I Coordinator/Elementary Supervisor
    105 Ruffin St.
    Emporia, VA 23847
    Phone: (434) 634-3748
    Website: http://www.pen.k12.va.us/Div/Greensville/

Harmony Hills Elementary School
    Barbara Hildreth, Principal
    Madelon K. Hickey Way
    Cohoes, NY 12047
    Phone: (518) 233-1900
    E-mail: bhildret@cohoes.org

Institute for Responsive Education
    Northeastern University
    40 Nightingale Hall
    Boston, MA 02115
    Phone: (617) 373-2595
    Website: http://www.dac.neu.edu/ire/home.html

Keshequa Central School District
    Ms. Lori Gray, PTSA President
    15 Mill St.
    Nunda, NY 14517
    Phone: (585) 476-2234, ext. 1213
    E-mail: dgraze@yahoo.com
    Website: http://www.kcs.k12.ny.us/default.htm

Living for the Young Family Through Education
    Joan Davis, Assistant Principal
    22 E. 128th St.
    New York, NY 10035
    Phone: (212) 831-1049

Lora B. Peck Elementary School
    Tameka Qualls, Project Manager
    Houston Independent School District
    5130 Arvilla
    Houston, TX 77021-2996
    Phone: (713) 845-7463

Mental Health in Schools Training and Technical Assistance Center
    UCLA/School Mental Health Project
    Department of Psychology
    P.O. Box 951563
    Los Angeles, CA 90095-1563
    Phone: (310) 825-3634
    E-mail: smhp@ucla.edu
    Website: http://www.smhp.psych.ucla.edu/

MetLife Foundation Teacher-Parent
Engagement Through Partnerships Initiative
National Coalition for Parent Involvement in Education
Website: www.ncpie.org

Middleburgh Central School District
John Metallo, Superintendent
181 Main Street
Middleburgh, NY 12122
Phone: (518) 827-5567
E-mail: metallo@rocketmail.com

Monica Leary Elementary School
Sue Mills, Principal
5509 E. Henrietta
Rush, NY 14543
Phone: (716) 359-5468
E-mail: smills@rhnet.org

National Center for Family and Community Connections with Schools
Emerging Issues in School, Family and Community Connections
Website: http://www.sedl.org/connections/resources/

National Center for Family and Community Connections with Schools
The Connection Collection: School–Family–Community
Connections Database
Website: http://www.sedl.org/connections/resources/

National Coalition for Parent Involvement in Education (NCPIE)
1201 16th St. NW, Box 39
Washington, DC 20036
Phone: (202) 822-8405
Website: http://www.ncpie.org

National Fatherhood Initiative
101 Lake Forest Boulevard, Suite 360
Gaithersburg, Maryland 20877
Phone: (301) 948-0599
Website: www.fatherhood.org

National Network of Partnership Schools
Johns Hopkins University
3003 N. Charles St., Suite 200
Baltimore, MD 21218
Phone: (410) 615-8818
E-mail: nnps@csos.jhu.edu
Website: http://222.partnershipschools.org

National Parent Teacher Association (PTA)
  330 North Wabash Ave.
  Suite 2100
  Chicago, IL 60611-3690
  Phone: (312) 670-6782
  E-mail: info@pta.org
  Website: www.pta.org

National Teacher Recruitment Clearinghouse
  Recruiting New Teachers
  385 Concord Ave., Suite 103
  Belmont, MA 02478
  Phone: (617) 489-6000
  Website: http://www.recruitingteachers.org/index.html

New City Elementary School
  Dorothy Atzl, Site Coordinator
  60 Crestwood Drive
  New City, NY 10956
  Phone: (845) 639-6360
  Website: http://www.ccsd.edu/newcity/

New York City Department of Youth and Community Development
  Beacon Programs
  New York, NY
  Phone: (212) 676-8255
  Website: http://www.ci.nyc.ny.us

Parent Partnership Network
  Michele Abdul Sabur, Parent Advocate
  Syracuse City School District
  725 Harrison St.
  Syracuse, NY 13210
  Phone: (315) 435-4148
  E-mail: mabdusab@freeside.scsd.k12.ny.us

The Partnership for Family Involvement in Education
  U.S. Department of Education
  400 Maryland Avenue, SW
  Washington, DC 20202-8173
  Phone: 1-800-USA-LEARN
  E-mail: partner@ed.gov
  Website: http://pfie.ed.gov

Ridgetop Elementary School
    Maria Teresa Flores
    Parent Involvement Coordinator
    5005 Caswell Ave.
    Austin, TX 78751
    Phone: (512) 414-4469
    Website: http://www.austinschools.org/ridgetop/

Rochester Action Center
    Barbara Jarzyniecki, Chief Communications Director
    30 Hart St.
    Rochester, NY 14605
    Phone: (716) 262-8070
    E-mail: Barbara.jarzyniecki@rcsdk12.org
    Website: http://www.rcsdk12.org/pac

Rush-Henrietta Central School District
    Rush-Henrietta Family Center
    Kay Lyons, Partnership School Facilitator
    Vollmer Building
    150 Telephone Road
    West Henrietta, NY
    Phone: (716) 359-7915 or 7912
    E-mail: Klyons@rhnet.org

University of Florida
    Dr. Jennifer M. Asmus
    Department of Educational Psychology
    P.O. Box 117047
    Gainesville, FL 32611-7047
    Phone: (352) 392-0723
    E-mail: Jasmus@coe.ufl.edu

University of Rochester
    Dr. Howard Kirschenbaum
    Warner Graduate School of Education and Human Development
    Rochester, NY 14627-0425
    Phone: (585) 275-5077
    E-mail: kirs@troi.cc.rochester.edu

University of Vermont
    Dr. Pam Key
    School Research Office
    Department of Education
    429 Waterman Building
    Burlington, VT 05405-0160
    Phone: (802) 656-8551
    E-mail: pkay@zoo.uvm.edu

Urbana Middle School
    Barbara Linder, Community Connections Coordinator
    West Campus
    1201 S. Vine
    Urbana, IL 61801
    Phone: (217) 337-0853
    E-mail: linderba@cmi.k12.il.us

Washington Irving High School
    Jenny Bailey, Program Director
    4 Irving Place
    New York, NY 10003
    Phone: (212) 358-1065

OTHER RESOURCES

WEBSITES

Connect for Success: Building a Teacher, Parent, Teen Alliance. National Teacher Recruitment Clearinghouse:
www.recruitingteachers.org/news/2002pitoolkit.html.

Family-school-community partnerships: A compilation of professional standards of practice for teachers. Harvard Family Research Project:
http://gseweb.harvard.edu.

Home school communication workshop. Harvard Family Research Project:
http://www.gse.harvard.edu/hfrp/projects/fine/resources/materials/home-school_workshop.html.

National PTA Model Parent Policy:
http://www.pta.org/programs/append.htm.

SCHOOL DISTRICT PARENT INVOLVEMENT POLICIES

Alexandria City, VA (Epstein, 2001).
Chaska, MN (Chaska Public Schools, 1989).
Chicago, IL (National PTA, Building Successful Partnerships, 2000).
Jefferson County, CO (Jefferson County, 2001).
Milwaukee, WI (Dietz, Resource 1–4, 1997).

Preparing Educators to Communicate and Connect with Families and Communities, pages 125–126

Montgomery County, MD (Epstein, 2001).
New York City, NY (2002).
San Diego, CA (Dietz, Resource 1–4, 1997).
Syracuse, NY (Epstein, 2001).
Tacoma, WA (Dietz, Resource 1–4, 1997).

STATE PARENT INVOLVEMENT POLICIES

California (Epstein, 2001).
Connecticut (Connecticut, 1998; Epstein, 2001).
Kentucky (Epstein, 2001).

RESOURCES FOR DESIGNING SCHOOL WEB PAGES

Designing Exemplary School Web Sites:
  http://www.caller2.com/grantms/schoolweb.html.

West Central Four Intermediate Service Agency:
  http://www.wc4.org/exemplaryschoolwebsites.htm.

VIDEOTAPES

Association for Supervision and Curriculum Development (Producer). (1992). Involving parents in education.
Bateman, B., & Kinney, T. (Producers). (2001). Emerging issues in special education. (Available from: Program Development Associates).
Bateman, B., & Kinney, T. (Producers). (2000). IEP success. (Available from: Attainment Company, Cicero, NY).
Cuellar, L., & Vaughn, C. (Producers). (1994). Latino parents as partners in education. (Available from Films for the Humanities and Science, Princeton, NJ).
Institute for Responsive Education (Producer). (1991). Building community: How to start a family center in your school.

RESOURCE GUIDE

Teens as Parents of Babies and Toddlers: A Resource Guide for Education. Cornell University Resource Center, Ithaca, NY 14850.

APPENDIX J

ADDITIONAL REFERENCES

Achieving Behaving Caring (ABC) Project. Burlington, VT: University of Vermont. Retrieved August 1, 2002, from: http://cecp.air.org/preventionstrategies/achievingbehavingcaring.htm.

Adams, K.C., & Christenson, S.L. (2000). Trust and the family-school relationship: Examination of parent-teacher differences in elementary and secondary grades. *Journal of School Psychology, 38,* 477–97.

Agosto, R. (1999, December). Community schools in New York City: The Board of Education and The Children's Aid Society. *NASSP Bulletin, 83*(611), 57–63.

Allexsaht-Snider, M. (1995). Teachers' perspectives on their work with families in a bilingual community. *Journal of Research in Childhood Education, 9*(2), 95–96.

Aronson, J.Z. (1996, April). How schools can recruit hard-to-reach parents. *Educational Leadership, 55*(8), 58–60.

Asmus, J.M., Vollmer, T.R., & Borrero, J.C. (2002, February). Functional behavioral assessment: A school-based model. *Education and Treatment of Children, 25*(1), 67–90.

Austin, T. (1994). *Changing the view: Student-led parent conferences.* Portsmouth, NH: Heinemann.

Ballen, J., & Moles, O. (1994). Strong families, strong schools. Washington, DC: U.S. Department of Education.

Balli, S.J. (1998). When Mom and Dad help: Student reflections on parent involvement with homework. *Journal of Research and Development in Education, 31*(3), 142–146.

Beale, A.V. (1999). Involving fathers in parent education: The counselor's challenge. *Professional School Counseling, 3*(1), 5–12.

Berger, E.H. (1995). *Parents as partners in education: Families and schools working together.* Englewood Cliffs, NJ: Merill.

Preparing Educators to Communicate and Connect with Families and Communities, pages 127–134
Copyright © 2005 by Information Age Publishing
All rights of reproduction in any form reserved.

Blackledge, A. (2000). *Literacy, power and social justice.* Staffordshire, England: Trentham Books Limited.

Blank, M.A., Kershaw, C. (1998). *The designbook for building partnerships: School, home, and community.* Lancaster, PA: Technomic Publishing Company.

Blank, M.J., & Langford, B.H. (2000). Strengthening partnerships: Community school assessment checklist. Washington, DC: Coalition for Community Schools.

Blank, M.J. & Langford, B.H. (2001, September). Strengthening partnerships: Community school assessment checklist. *Principal Leadership, 2*(1), 62–63.

Bloom, L.R. "I'm poor, I'm single, I'm a mom, and I deserve respect": Advocating in school as/with mothers in poverty. *Education Studies, 32*(3), 300–316.

Borba, J.A., & Olvera, C.M. (2001, July/August). Student-led parent-teacher conferences. *The Clearing House, 74*(6), 333–336.

Bryk, A.S., & Schneider, B. (2002). *Trust in schools: A core resource for improvement.* New York: Russell Sage Foundation.

Bureau of the Census. (1997). *How we're changing: Demographic state of the nation. 1996.* Current Population Reports, Special Studies Series. Washington, DC: U.S. Department of Commerce.

Buttery, T.J., & Anderson, P.J. (1999, Fall). Community, school, and parent dynamics: A synthesis of literature and activities. *Teacher Education Quarterly, 26*(4), 111–122.

Canter, L., & Canter, M. (1991). *Parents on your side.* Santa Monica, CA: Lee Canter & Associates.

Caplan, J. (2001). *Essential for principals: Strengthening the connection between school and home.* Alexandria, VA: National Association of Elementary School Principals.

Carter, S. (2002). *The impact of parent/family involvement on student outcomes: An annotated bibliography of research during the past decade.* Eugene, OR: Consortium for Appropriate Dispute Resolution in Special Education (CADRE).

Casper, V., & Schultz, S.B. (1999). *Gay parents/straight schools: Building communication and trust.* New York: Teachers College, Columbia University.

Chaska Public Schools. (1989). *Parent partnership policy.* Chaska, MN: Author. Retrieved July 31, 2002 from http://www.ncrel.org.

Children's Aid Society. (2001). *Building a community school* (3rd ed.). New York: Author. Retrieved August 16, 2002 from: http://www.childrensaidsociety.org.

Christenson, S.L., & Sheridan, S.M. (2001). *Schools and families: Creating essential connections for learning.* New York: Guilford Press.

Christopher, C.J. (1996). *Building parent-teacher communication: An educator's guide.* Lancaster, PA: Technomic.

Clemens-Brower, T.J. (1997, February). Recruiting parents and the community. *Educational Leadership, 54,* 58–60.

Connor, C. (2000). Rebuilding a parent program with technology. *Principal, 80*(1), 61–62.

Cooper, H.M., Lindsay, J.J., & Nye, B. (2000). Homework in the home: How student, family, and parenting-style differences relate to the homework process. *Contemporary Educational Psychology, 25*(4), 464–487.

Countryman, G., Donielson, S., & Eggleston, D. (1994). *Parent involvement in education: A resource for parents, educators, and communities.* Des Moines: Iowa Department of Education.

Covarrubia, J. (2000). Family literacy: Sharing classrooms with parents. *Principal, 80*(1), 44–45.

Davern, L. (1996, April). Listening to parents of children with disabilities. *Educational Leadership, 53*(7), 61–63.

Davis, B. (1995). *How to involve parents in a multicultural school.* Alexandria, VA: Association for Supervision and Curriculum Development.

Decker, L.E. (2001, September). Allies in education. *Principal Leadership, 2*(1), 42–26.

DiCamillo, M.P. (2001). Parent education as an essential component of parent involvement programs. In D.B. Hiatt-Michael (Ed.), *Promising practices for family involvement in schools* (pp. 153–183). Greenwich, CT: Information Age Publishing.

Dietz, M.J. (1997). *School, family and community: Techniques and models for successful collaboration.* Gaithersburg, MD: Aspen Publishers.

Dodd, A.W., & Konzal, J.L. (2002). *How communities build stronger schools: Stories, strategies, and promising practices for educating every child.* New York: Palgrave Macmillan.

Drake, D.D. (2000). Parents and families as partners in the education process: Collaboration for the success of students in public schools. *ERS Spectrum,* 34–35.

Dryfoos, J. (1996, April). Full-service schools. *Educational Leadership, 53,* 18–23.

Dryfoos, J. (2002, January). Full-service community schools: Creating new institutions. *Phi Delta Kappan, 83*(5), 393–399.

Dryfoos, J., & Maguire, S. (2002). *Inside full-service community schools.* Thousand Oaks, CA: Corwin Press.

Durkin, R., & Jarney, M. (2001, September). Staying after school-And loving it. *Principal Leadership, 2*(1), 50–53.

Eber, L. (1999, Fall). *Family voice, teacher voice. Claiming Children,* p. 10. ECS Information Clearinghouse. (2002). 2000-01 selected state policies. Denver, CO: Education Commission of the States. Retrieved September 12, 2002, from: www.ecs.org.

Edwards, P.A., Fear, K.L., & Galego, M.A. (1995). Role of parents in responding to issues of linguistic and cultural diversity. In E.E. Garcia, B. McLaughlin, B. Spodek, and O. Saracho (Eds.), *Meeting the challenge of linguistic and cultural diversity in early childhood education* (pp. 141–153). New York: Teachers College Press.

Epstein, J.L. (1987). Toward a theory of family-school connections. Teacher practices and parent involvement. In K. Hurrelmann, F. Kaufmann, and F. Losel (Eds.), *Social Interventions: Potential and constraints* (pp. 121–136). New York: DeGruyter.

Epstein, J.L. (1995). School, family, community partnerships: Caring for the children we share. *Phi Delta Kappan, 77,* 701–712.

Epstein, J.L. (2001). *School, family, and community partnerships: Preparing educators and improving schools.* Boulder, CO: Westview Press.

Epstein, J.L., & Clark, L.A. (2000). *Budgets and funding research brief.* Baltimore, MD: National Network of Partnership Schools. Retrieved August 7, 2002 from: http://www.csos.jhu.edu/p2000.brief.htm.

Epstein, J.L., Coates, L., Salinas, K.C., Sanders, M.G., & Simon, B. (1997). *School, family and community partnerships: Your handbook for action.* Thousand Oaks, CA: Corwin Press.

Family as faculty. (2000, Fall). *FINE Forum e-Newsletter.* Retrieved September 5, 2002, from: http://www.gse.harvard.edu/hfrp/projects/fine/fineforum/index.html.

Finders, M. & Lewis, C. (1994). Why some parents don't come to school. *Educational Leadership, 51*(8), 50–54.

France, M.G., & Hager, J.M. (1993). Recruit, respect, respond: A model for working with low-income families and their preschoolers. *The Reading Teacher, 46,* 568–572.

Freedman, E., & Montgomery, J.F. (1994). Parent education and student achievement. *Thrust for Educational Leadership, 24,* 40–44.

Fresno Unified School District. (2002). *Parent mobile.* Retrieved August 19, 2002, from: www.fresno.k12.ca.us/divdept/pec/parmobl.html.

Fruchter, N., Galleta, A., and White, J.L. (1992). *New directions in parent involvement.* Washington, DC: Academy for Educational Development.

Fuller, M.L., & Olsen, G. (1998). *Home-school relations: Working successfully with parents and families.* Boston: Allyn and Bacon.

Garriott, P.O., Wandry, D., & Snyder, L. (2002, Fall). Teachers as parents, parents as children: What's wrong with this picture? *Preventing School Failure, 45*(1), 37–43.

Giannetti, C.C., & Sagarese, M.M. (1997). *The roller-coaster years: Raising your child through the maddening yet magical middle school years.* New York: Broadway Books.

Giannetti, C.C., & Sagarese, M.M. (1998, May). Turning parents from critics to allies. *Educational Leadership, 55*(8), 40–42.

Gustafson, C. (1998, October). Phone home. *Educational Leadership, 56*(2), 31–32.

Henderson, A.T., Marburger, C.L., & Ooms, T. (1986). *Beyond the bake sale: An educator's guide to working with parents.* Columbia, MD: National Committee for Citizens in Education.

Henderson, A.T., & Raimondo, B.N. (2001). Unlocking parent potential. *Principal Leadership, 2*(1), 27–32.

Hiatt-Michael, D.B. (2001). *Preparing teachers to work with parents.* Washington, DC: ERIC Clearinghouse on Teaching and Teacher Education. (ERIC Digest #460123). Retrieved July 18, 2002, from: http://www.ericsp.org.

Hiatt-Michael, D.B. (Ed.). (2001). *Promising practices for family involvement in schools.* Greenwich, CT: Information Age Publishing.

Hoover-Dempsey, K.V., & Sandler, H.M. (1995). Parents' reported involvement in students' homework: Strategies and practices. *Elementary School Journal, 95*(5), 435–450.

Hoover-Dempsey, K.V., Battaito, A.C., Walker, J.M.T., Reed, R.P., DeJong, J.M., and Jones, K.P. (2001). Parental involvement in homework. *Educational Psychologist, 36*(3), 195–209.

Hornby, G. (2000). *Improving parental involvement.* New York: Cassell.

Huff, B. (1999, Fall). Collaborating with schools. *Claiming Children,* p. 1.

Hurd, T.L., Lerner, R.M., & Barton, C.D. (1999). Integrated services: Expanding partnerships to meet the needs of today's children and families. *Young Children, 54*(2), 74–80.

Imelli, G., & Purvis, J. (2000, September). Web wonder: Connecting parents and teachers. *Media and Methods, 37*(1), 8–9.

Jesse, D. (1995). Increasing parental involvement: A key to student achievement. In Mid-continent Regional Educational Laboratory, *What's noteworthy on learners, learning, schooling* (pp. 19–26).

Johnson, V.R. (2000). The family center: Making room for parents. *Principal, 80*(11), 26–31.

Johnson, V.R. (2001). Family centers in schools. In D.B. Hiatt-Michael (Ed.), *Promising practices for family involvement in schools* (pp. 85–106). Greenwich, CT: Information Age Publishing.

Kay, P.J., & Fitzgerald, M. (1997, Sept/Oct). Parents+teachers+action research=real involvement. *Teaching Exceptional Children, 30,* 8–11.

Kirschenbaum, H. (2001). Educating professionals for school, family and community partnerships. In D.B. Hiatt-Michael (Ed.), *Promising practices for family involvement in schools* (pp. 185–206). Greenwich, CT: Information Age Publishing.

Kugler, E. (2002). *Debunking the middle class myth: Why diverse schools are good for all kids.* Lanham, NJ: Scarecrow Press.

Kyle, D.W., McIntyre, E., Miller, K.B., & Moore, G.H. (2002). *Reaching out: A K–8 resource for connecting families and schools.* Thousand Oaks, CA: Corwin Press.

Lake, J. (2000). An analysis of factors that contribute to parent-school conflict in specialeducation. *Remedial & Special Education, 21*(4), 240–252.

Lake, R. (1998). Caught between two worlds. In Editorial Projects in Education (Ed.), *Thoughtful teachers, thoughtful schools* (3rd ed.) (pp. 123–125). Boston: Allyn and Bacon.

Lian, M.J., & Fontanez-Phelan, S.M. (2001). Perceptions of Latino parents regarding cultural and linguistic issues and advocacy for children with disabilities. *Journal of the Association for Persons with Severe Handicaps, 26*(3), 189–194.

Lindsay, J.W., & Enright, S.G. (1997). *Books, babies, and school-age parents: How to teach pregnant and parenting teens to succeed.* Buena Park, CA: Morning Glory Press.

Little, A.W. & Allan, J. (1989). Student led parent-teacher conferences. *Elementary School Guidance and Counseling, 23*(3), 210–221.

Leuder, D.C. (1998). *Creating partnerships with parents: An educator's guide.* Lancaster, PA: Technomic Publishing Co.

Lynch, E.W., & Hanson, M.J. (1998). *Developing cross-cultural competence: A guide for working with children and their families.* Baltimore: Paul H. Brookes.

Marchant, G.J., Sharon, E.P., & Rothlisberg, B.A. (2001). Relations of middle school students' perceptions of family and school contexts with academic achievement. *Psychology in the Schools, 38*(6), 505–519.

Mayhew, C. (2001). *Family support services in New York State for children with emotional and behavioral disabilities and their families.* Albany, NY: Families Together in New York State, Inc.

Melaville, A., & Blank, M.J. (1998). *Learning together: The developing field of school-community initiatives.* Flint, MI: Mott Foundation.

Muscott, H.S. (2002, Winter). Exceptional partnerships: Listening to the voices of families. *Preventing School Failure, 46*(2), 66–69.

New City Family Resource Center. (2000). New City, NY: New City Elementary School. Retrieved August 29, 2002, from: http://www.ccsd.edu/newcity/.

National Coalition for Parent Involvement in Education. (2002). *Building family-school partnerships that work.* Retrieved August 20, 2002, from: http://www.ncpie.org.

National PTA. (1999). *National PTA national standards for parent/family involvement programs.* Retrieved August 2, 2002, from: http://www.pta.org/programs/appena.htm.

National PTA. (2000). *Building successful partnerships: A guide for developing parent and family involvement programs.* Bloomington, IN: National Education Service.

Onikama, D.L., Hammond, O.W., & Koki, S. (1998). *Family involvement in education: A synthesis of research for Pacific educators.* Honolulu, HI: Pacific Resources for Education and Learning.

O'Shea, D.J., O'Shea, L.J., Algozzine, R., & Hammitte, D.J. (2001). *Families and teachers of individuals with disabilities: Collaborative orientations and responsive practices.* Boston: Allyn and Bacon.

Patrikako, E.N. (1997, Fall). A model of parental attitudes and academic achievement of adolescents. *Journal of Research and Development in Education, 31,* 7–26.

Patten, P. (2002), March-May). Parent involvement in middle school: The story of one school. An interview with Barbara Linder. *Parent News.* Retrieved December 2, 2002, from: http://www.npin.org.

Payne, R.K. (2001). *A framework for understanding poverty.* Highlands, TX: aha! Process, Inc.

Power, B. (1999). *Parent power: Energizing home-school communication.* Portsmouth, NH: Heinemann.

Power, B. (1999, October). Strengthen your parent connection. *Instructor, 109*(3), 30–1.

Reay, D. (1998). Classifying feminist research: Exploring the psychological impact of social class on mothers' involvement in children's schooling. *Feminism and Psychology 8*(2), 155–171.

Reay, D. (1999). Linguistic capital and home-school relationships: Mothers' interactions with their primary school teachers. *Acta Sociologica 42*(2), 159–168.

Reyes, P., Scribner, J.D. & Scribner, A.P. (Eds.). (1999). *Lessons from high performing Hispanic schools: Creating learning communities.* New York: Teachers College Press.

Rice, R. (1998, Winter). Preparing teachers to work with families and communities. *Family, School, Community Partnerships,* 3–4.

Rich, D. (1998, May). What parents want from teachers. *Educational Leadership, 55*(8), 36–38.

Robbins, P. (1995). *The principal's companion: Strategies and hints to make the job easier.* Thousand Oaks, CA: Corwin Press.

Rochester City School District. (2002). *Parent Action Center Exit Survey.* Retrieved August 12, 2002, from: http://www.rcsdk12.org/pac.

Rockwell, R.E., Andrew, L.C., & Hawley, M.K. (1996). *Parents and teachers as partners: Issues and challenges.* Orlando: Harcourt Brace & Company.

Rosenthal, D.M., & Sawyers, J.Y. (1996). Building successful home/school partnerships. *Childhood Education, 72*(4), 194–200.

Ryan, A.K., Kay, P.J., Fitzgerald, M., Paquette, S., & Smith, S. (2001). Kyle: A case study in parent-teacher action research. *Teaching Exceptional Children, 33*(3), 56–61.

Salinas, K.C. Jansom, N.R., & Nolan, J. (Eds.). (2001). *Promising partnership practices 2001.* Baltimore: Center on School, Family, and Community Partnerships, Johns Hopkins University. Retrieved June 17, 2002, from: http://www.csos .jhu.edu/p2000/publications.htm.

Shartrand, A.M., Weiss, H.B., Kreider, H.M., & Lopez, M.E. (1997). *New skills for new schools: Preparing teachers in family involvement.* Cambridge, MA: Harvard Family Research Project. Retrieved July 16, 2002, from: http://www.ed.gov/pubs/ NewSkills/title.html.

Simon, B.S. (2001). Family involvement in high school: Predictors and effects. *NASSP Bulletin, 85*(627), 8–19.

Singer, G.H.S. & Powers, L.E. (1993). *Families, disability, and empowerment: Active coping skills and strategies for family interventions.* Baltimore, MD: Paul H. Brookes.

Stayton, V., & Miller, P. (1993). Personal competence. In DEC Task Force on Recommended Practices, *DEC recommended practices: Indicators of quality in programs for infants and young children with special needs and their families.* Reston, VA: Council for Exceptional Children.

Stone, R. (1999). *Best classroom practices: What award-winning elementary teachers do.* Thousand Oaks, CA: Corwin Press, Inc.

Strickland, J.S., & Chan, T.C. (2001, September). A powerful tool for parent-school communication. *Principal Leadership, 2*(1), 81–82.

Sui-Chi, E.H., & Willms, J.D. (1996, April). Effects of parental involvement on eighth-grade achievement. *Sociology of Education, 69,* 126–141.

Swap, S.M. (1993). *Developing home-school partnerships: From concepts to practice.* New York: Teachers' College, Columbia University.

Syracuse City School District Partnership Policy. In Epstein, J.L. (2001), *School, family and community partnerships: Preparing educators and improving schools* (pp. 332–333). Boulder, CO: Westview Press.

Thompson, S. (1993). Two streams, one river. Parent involvement and teacher empowerment. *Equity and Choice, 101,* 17–20.

Thorp, E.K. (1997, May). Increasing opportunities for partnership with culturally and linguistically diverse families. *Intervention in School and Clinic, 32,* 261–269.

Trumbull, E., Rothstein-Fisch, C., Greenfield, P.M., & Quiroz, B. (2001). *Bridging cultures between home and school: A guide for teachers.* Mahwah, New Jersey: Lawrence Erlbaum Associates.

Turnbull, A.P., & Turnbull, H.R. (1997). *Families, professionals, and exceptionality: A special partnership* (3rd ed.). Upper Saddle River, NJ: Prentice-Hall, Inc.

Turnbull, A.P., Turnbull, H.R., Shank, M., & Leal, D. (1995). *Exceptional lives: Special education in today's schools.* Englewood Cliffs, NH: Merrill/Prentice Hall.

U.S. Department of Education. (1994). Personal conversation with teachers in the shadow teacher program at the U.S. Department of Education, Washington, DC.

Wehmeyer, M., Sands, D.J., Knowlton, H.E., & Kozleski, E.B. (2002). *Teaching students with mental retardation: Providing access to the general curriculum.* Baltimore: Paul H. Brookes.

Whitaker, T., & Fiore, D.J. (2001). *Dealing with difficult parents (and with parents in difficult situations).* Larchmont, NY: Eye on Education.

Wollman-Bonilla, J. (2000). *Family message journals: Teaching writing through family involvement.* Urbana, IL: National Council of Teachers of English.

Zardoya, I. (2001). Urban students cross the digital divide through laptop leasing program. *Education, 122*(2), 262–268.

ABOUT THE CONTRIBUTORS

Ellen Chernoff, MA, M.Ed., a graduate of SUNY Buffalo, continued her professional preparation at UT San Antonio, as a Title VII fellow in bilingual education. She was awarded resources and accepted into the bilingual educational diagnostician program at Bank Street College. As an educator for over 20 years she has worked as a bilingual teacher, an educational diagnostician, and a staff developer. Currently she is a bilingual professional development specialist with Special Education Training and Resource Center in upstate NY.

Patricia A. Edwards, a literacy professor at Michigan State University, is the 2006 President-Elect of the National Reading Conference. She is a world-renowned researcher, as well as a recognized outstanding teacher, with numerous articles and chapters in the most prestigious journals and books. Furthermore, her most recent book, *Children's Literacy Development: Making it Happen through School, Family, and Community Involvement* (2004) has added significantly to the field of literacy learning and academic achievement in high poverty areas.

Amanda Fenlon is an Assistant Professor of Special Education in the Curriculum and Instruction Department at SUNY Oswego. She has been a special education teacher, administrator and director of early intervention programs. Current research interests include partnerships with parents of students with disabilities and the development of inclusive extended school year programs.

Preparing Educators to Communicate and Connect with Families and Communities, pages 135–136
Copyright © 2005 by Information Age Publishing
135

Grace Ibanez-Friedman began her life as a professional educator in preschool teaching. She received her doctorate from Rutgers University and pursued research in teacher development and parental involvement. More specifically, she uses action research methodology to document changes in teacher cognition, behavior, and practice. Presently, she is an assistant professor in the Department of Early Childhood, Childhood and Adolescent Education at St. Johns University.

Diane J. Heller, a 1980 graduate of Cornell University in the College of Industrial and Labor Relations, completed her internship in Rio de Janeiro, Brasil and then returned to the USA as a caseworker for Child Protective Services. Most of Ms. Heller's work was with parents and children with special physical and mental needs. Her husband, Michael Milholland, works in a night shelter for men, and sons Evan and Wyatt are involved in the arts.

Peter Kozik, a former K – 12 Principal and Director of Special Education, is currently a project assistant/research coordinator for the New York Higher Education Support Center for Systems Change and a doctoral candidate at Syracuse University. In addition to family engagement, his current research interests include student empowerment and school board policy making.

Tracy Knight Lackey, a former special educator, is currently an Assistant Professor in the Department of Teaching and Leadership at Syracuse University. The crux of her work is the experience of families rearing children with disabilities and incarcerated youth with disabilities. She and her husband Hilliard have one son, Cinco.

Marybeth A. Schillace is a New York State certified teacher for the New York State Department of Correctional Services. She completed Graduate coursework in Education at Le Moyne College, earned a B.A. in English from Fairfield University, and an M.A. in Public Relations from the S.I. Newhouse School of Public Communications at Syracuse University. She and her husband, and their three children live in the Finger Lakes region of New York.

Patricia Ruggiano Schmidt is a literacy professor at Le Moyne College, Syracuse, New York. Her ethnographic research takes her into urban classrooms where she studies culturally responsive pedagogy and has authored numerous books, book chapters, and journal articles. She believes her most important contribution to education is to prepare present and future teachers for understanding and appreciating diverse populations through her model known as the ABC's of Cultural Understanding and Communication.

CPSIA information can be obtained
at www.ICGtesting.com
Printed in the USA
LVHW080110040119
602733LV00004B/27/P